WHO
AND
WHY
YOU
ARE

All you need to remember

ROLAND ACHENJANG, PHARM.D., MBA

Contents

I dedicate this book to you, you brave soul. Your contributions to the current Earth life experience are responsible for creating this special moment — a moment in which you are reading this sentence; in which you are reading this book. And for that, I am eternally grateful (I know Consciousness is, too). Read it with joy as you remember more and more of who and why you truly are.

Waleed —
Unconditional love is
yours to Experience &
Share with the world!

Epigram

You are simple; you are complex. You are everything; you are nothing. But you *are*! And that you are, is enough! It's more than enough.

Acknowledgements

See book dedication ☺

Preface

It felt like my day at work lasted longer than it had on most other days. As soon as my shift ended, I left and began my walk home. The noise, commotion, and bustling activity of people rushing to work or to a doctor's appointment early in the mornings had become background noise during my commute. Even noises produced by birds chirping had faded away and found a resting place in the backdrop of my conscious awareness. My perception of the noise produced by this morning's activities was no different. I walked slowly with my head facing down and only looked up to ensure my safety before crossing road intersections. Looking down also provided me an illusionary escape from the sun's rays as it began to make itself visible through the morning clouds. Eight minutes after I left work, I was home.

I tidied up by putting away my work items, took a warm shower, and sluggishly made my way to my bedroom, where I sat on the edge of my bed. Even with wide open eyes, I could barely see anything in my room or any part of my body. I had invested in very effective blackout curtains that were draped over my bedroom window. I loved how reliable they were at blocking out the light and heat produced by the sun. Blocking the sunlight was not my preference, and instead, a necessity since I worked the graveyard shifts at a very large hospital in midtown Nashville, Tennessee. I needed the darkness and colder room temperatures to help me sleep through the day.

It had been two years since I'd begun working the graveyard shift. Every other week, I felt jet lagged. I had come to a point where I was obliged to find a creative solution to adjust to the back-and-forth, week-in-and-week-out schedule, because it had become extremely harsh on my body. I felt tired, weary, and exhausted all the time and my cognition and overall mood deteriorated. At the same time, I had begun to grow frustrated with not finding answers to the universal truths and meanings of life—answers I had begun to search for when I was eight years old.

See, growing up in Cameroon, West Africa, I was raised in the Catholic faith. I never felt fully comfortable with some of its teachings and found others to be contradictory. Through the years, I developed the same feelings towards other religions I learned about. Their subtle practices of exclusion, or perpetuating the notion of only one way to finding salvation, never fully resonated with me. Besides my ever-growing skepticisms with religions, the unfairnesses I perceived in the world were difficult to accept. Suffering, diseases, violence, bullying, and death fascinated me, in a painful way. My limited understandings of these experiences, coupled with not finding the answers to the questions I began searching for when I was eight years old, and working the graveyard shift and dealing with its own challenges, resulted in my life becoming a grey experience. Funnily enough, since for over two years I seldom saw the sunlight, I began to welcome and appreciate the darkness.

I spent countless hours alone in the dark, thinking about my past experiences. Many colorful, fond memories would arise from deep within my subconscious, teasing me. Looking back, I appreciate how these memories were a beacon of hope for me. They reminded me that it was possible to experience Earth life from another perspective—one filled with color and excitement. The biggest challenge for me was figuring out a solution to realizing and maintaining these perspectives and feelings again. My attempts often led me back to the silence and solitude of my dark bedroom, which is where I found myself this morning.

After sitting on the edge of my bed, I let my hands rest on my thighs and thought a while about what I was getting ready to do. Honestly, I had looked forward to this moment and had thought much about it when I'd had some downtime at work earlier that night. This is why my shift that night felt longer than most others. This was additionally a special moment for me, and I need you to understand why. It had been a good while since I experienced a moment I anticipated with excitement.

Anyway, with my hands on my thighs and feet flat on the floor, I slowly closed my eyes and inhaled deeply, then exhaled. The exhale was slow and deep, and represented having nothing else to lose, and, therefore, deciding in that moment to embark on this new experience with everything I had to offer —with all of me. After exhaling, I began observing and listening to my breath, my heart rate, different parts of my body, and my thoughts.

In the hours and days leading up to this moment, the idea of listening to my being came to me as a potential solution for getting out of the grey world that had become my Earth life experience. Nothing else I had tried up to this moment had succeeded, so this was another attempt. And similar to how I questioned most things in life as far back as I can remember, I became curious about and interested in the thought (of listening to my body). I became eager to find out what would happen if I simply listened to my being. I wondered what I would learn or experience if I sat in silence and observed every part of me— my thoughts, autonomic nervous system, parts of my body, and body movements. I had never done anything like this before.

Interestingly, after mulling over the idea in the days leading to this moment, I began to feel sad for neglecting my body and mind for over twenty-eight years. This was particularly troubling because I have always had access to both. The sad feeling peaked on this morning when I sat on the edge of my bed and right after my exhale. I felt slightly comforted knowing that my actions were the beginning of the end of me ignoring myself.

So, for the first time in my life, sitting in my bedroom void of sunlight granted me by the blackout curtains hanging over my bedroom windows, exhausted but with enough energy to also be partly excited, with my eyes shut, hands on my thighs and feet flat on the floor, and with every part of my being, I meditated. As far as I can remember, I meditated for no more than five minutes before falling into deep sleep from physical exhaustion. Still, I had done it.

Nothing exciting or out of the ordinary happened to me during this first session. I wasn't even sure that what I did was meditating. It was only after waking up that I laid in my bed and tried again. During the late afternoon session, I identified with the countless thoughts racing through my mind and noticed that I quickly switched from one thought to another. This went on for about ten minutes or so, before my responsibilities forced me to stop. I had to wake up and prepare for school and work.

I had no idea that the thought to bring awareness to my physical being and mind chatter, and the decision to act on it would turn out to be the beginning of the most beautiful adventure I have ever experienced. At the time of this writing, it has been a four-year adventure that, to this day, continues to provided me tremendous insight into who and why I am. I am gaining profound understandings about how my mind works, what my emotions are and where they come from, and why I behave the way I do. The icing on the cake is, I truly believe these understandings are universal. They are just as true for you as they are for me.

Further, my meditating practices continue to provide me with experiences I often find difficult to describe with words. I have come to accept they can only be experienced to be fully understood or appreciated by anyone else. Meditating continues to teach me the importance of being present in every moment in my life, regardless of what I am experiencing or how challenging I perceive the situation to be. Meditating helps me appreciate minute but significant changes taking place within and on the surface of my physical body.

As a pharmacist with a strong scientific background, I would have been skeptical if someone tried to introduce the notion of one being able to improve their overall health, well-being, and physicality by meditating. Today, I write from my personal experience that this is entirely possible, and much more. I continue to meditate every day, and the practice is still providing me access to an infinite amount of healing, knowledge, wisdom, and creativity.

Without a doubt, meditating, or the act of focusing my conscious awareness on my entire being, is the only practice I engage in that provides me answers to what I began searching for when I was eight years old. Meditating provides me answers to the universal truths about who and why we are, and the purpose and meaning of life on Earth. I am eternally grateful that I began remembering this information very early on the lovely morning of Tuesday August 21st, 2018. Nothing about my being, perceptions, and earthly experiences have been the same since.

What to Expect

———————

This book is based on my personal experiences, perceptions, and current awareness of who and why we all are. I believe these to be universal truths. In the book, I do my best to explain the truths, concepts, and understandings I introduce, believing they will grant you many opportunities to also remember them. The information can also provide you with valuable insight into how you can make your Earth life a more relaxed and joyful experience.

The book is set up in three parts. In the first part of the book, creatively titled Part I, I present information to help you remember and understand **who** you are. I have done my best to make this simple.

In the second part of the book, also creatively title Part II, I present information to help you remember **why** you are. Part II constitutes the bulk of the book, because understanding why you are requires more explanations. I split the second part in to two sub-parts, parts II-A and II-B. In part II-A, I focus on why you are experiencing life on Earth and provide the universal truths that support my understanding. In part II-B, I focus on why experiencing life on Earth is beneficial for you after you transition from this current incarnation.

I want you to know that understanding the entirety of who and why you are is actually very simple, and I promise you will laugh out loud in the moment that you remember. I did.

In the last part of the book, Part III, I include my most effective and go-to methods or tools, and other valuable resources you can use anywhere and at any time to help you remember who and why you are. Not only are some of the tools and methods free, you also already have all the skills and abilities to do them. The most important takeaway from this section is that you use the tools and do the practices.

I would be sad if I did not take this moment to let you know there is no one right way to remember these universal truths, and what I share is limited to my experiences. Truth is, you will inevitably remember, whether in this lifetime or another, and most definitely after you die. Countless souls throughout mankind's history on Earth have employed multiple means to remember these same universal truths. Instead of focusing your energy chasing the next fad, I implore you to be consistent with a practice that is unique to you, and that you find enjoyable.

There is a story in the Bible that discusses "Master Jesus" teaching his followers about the importance of consistency. In the story, Master Jesus explained that only few people would find life because the road that leads to it is narrow and the gate guarding it is small. In other words, consistency will provide you with your most significant opportunities for personal growth and for remembering these universal truths.

By the way, I call Jesus Christ "Master Jesus" because I believe he understood these same universal truths and his teachings were his attempts to explain them while he was incarnate on Earth. In effect, he was a teacher, and a great teacher he was. He was a master in his understandings, application, and ability to explain this knowledge. You know, there have been many such teachers incarnate on Earth over the years. Siddhartha Gautama, commonly known as the Buddha, was one such soul. So, because Jesus held a high degree of understanding of this information, I refer to him as Master Jesus.

Interpretations Are Your Own Only

I am confident you are aware of how personal beliefs and environmental influences cause people to experience miscommunications and misunderstandings. I am confident you can recount personal experiences in your life when your word choices and or beliefs led to embarrassing, comical, or even catastrophic interactions with others. If you have been so fortunate as to have never experienced this first-hand, you can examine what has resulted from different people's readings and interpretations of the metaphoric verses in the Bible.

Now, please know that I am in no way comparing this book to the Bible. I have no intention of writing a metaphoric book about who and why we are. However, I do present this point to help you appreciate how interpretations of the written word might stray from the author's intentions. This is true, and this book will be subject to the same reality. It is inevitable that someone else reading this book will ascertain a different message from it than you or even me. This is perfectly fine, and I expect it to occur.

To remedy this problem and help you instead focus on the overarching message (and not the choice of words), I include scenarios, examples, or situations that describe the concepts I present. Some of them will be made-up stories, based on my personal experiences or mainstream information. Others will require you to assess how you will act or react if you found yourself in the hypothetical situations. This will require you to be creative, and I ask that you are always honest in your assessments and decisions on the behaviors you choose to act on. I know you are infinitely creative, and that makes me believe you will do great no matter the scenario or situation. You will also learn something about who you truly are and might even surprise yourself in the process!

Now that you are fully in the know about what to expect, I would like to take this opportunity to ask that you accept my sincere appreciation and gratitude that you've chosen to read this book. It means the world to me!

Read it with joy.

Enjoy!

Connection to Consciousness Assessment

Everything you currently believe about who and why you are, and your current assessment of your personal life and the world at large, is directly related to your current level of awareness of your connection to Consciousness, or Oneness. What you currently believe, or your current perceptions of who and why you are, provides you altered understandings of the truths about who you truly are and why you truly are. These altered understandings are neither right nor wrong. Again, they merely reflect your current level of awareness of your connection to Consciousness.

As you read through this book, your understandings will change. They will change not solely because you read this book, but also because you continue to experience life on Earth. It is inevitable that this happens. In fact, this has been happening to you throughout your entire earthly existence, unfortunately, without your conscious awareness. As your understandings change, so will your awareness of your connection to Consciousness. Beginning today, I encourage you to track the changes by using the simple assessment tool I created below. Use the results from you first assessment as a benchmark for you going forward.

You may complete the assessment as many times as you like while reading this book. I recommend that after completing it (the assessment) today, you at a minimum, complete it again when you finish reading the book. You may also return to the assessment at any time in your life should you feel the need. There are no limits to how often you can take it.

To accurately assess your personal growth and reap the benefits of this assessment, it is worthwhile that you always answer the questions honestly. Do not worry; there is no right or wrong answer!

Self-Awareness Assessment

On a scale from one to ten, how content are you with who you are as a person, considering everything good/heavenly about you and everything bad/hellish about you, in this moment?

1   2   3   4   5   6   7   8   9   10

Disgusted   Perfectly Content

Is there anything about you that you do not like and want to change in this moment?

YES   NO

If you answered **YES** to the question above, do you believe you cannot change the thing beginning from this moment?

YES   NO

World-Awareness Assessment

On a scale from one to ten, how content are you with the current state of the world, considering everything good/heavenly about it and everything bad/hellish about it, in this moment?

1   2   3   4   5   6   7   8   9   10

Disgusted   Perfectly Content

Is there anything about the world that you do not like and want to change in this moment?

YES   NO

If you answered **YES** to the question above, do you believe you cannot change the thing beginning from this moment?

YES   NO

Part I:
Who You Are

1

You Are Consciousness

"Although you appear in Earthly form, your essence is pure Consciousness." —Rumi

onsciousness is not only alive, but it is also the most basic and fundamental essence of every single thing that exists. Also, Consciousness as it is in its current form is always perfect! This is true, and since it is true, every single thing that exists throughout the cosmos, as it does in its current form, is a unique form of Consciousness and is always perfect! Put another way, since Consciousness is everything, this means nothing—whether living or dead, organic or inorganic, visible to the naked eye or otherwise— exists that is separate from or outside of Consciousness. What I mean by that is Consciousness or Oneness is All That Is. At this point, you might be confused about what you just read, and I appreciate that; however, I am not giving up on helping you remember this essential and universal truth, as it is necessary for you to remember who you are.

So, consider this other explanation:

Every single thing that exists throughout the cosmos is a form of energy vibrating at a unique frequency. You can affect your perception of this existing form of energy by changing its frequency of vibration. This is true regardless of how the energy exists. If the form of energy exists in a physical nature, understand that you can only cause the energy to change from one form of physical presentation to another, by changing its frequency of vibration. You can never destroy the energy. I can bet you remember this information, or something similar, from your introductory classes in the sciences.

Building on this knowledge of everything that exists throughout the cosmos being energy vibrating at a unique frequency, consider that if Consciousness, or Oneness, is also everything, and everything is a form of energy vibrating at some unique frequency, Consciousness or Oneness must be a type of energy. Simply put, Consciousness or Oneness is Energy.

Now, if Consciousness is Energy, then every single thing that exists must be a unique expression of Energy, differing solely on the frequency of the Energy's vibration. This is true, and I hope I have not lost you yet. If you feel lost, please return and read from the beginning before proceeding. If you are not lost, feel free to proceed, knowing you are closer to remembering who you are.

No one and nothing ever creates new Energy, Consciousness, or Oneness; however, by combining different quantities of different unique expressions of Energy, Consciousness, or Oneness, and subjecting the combination to differing external forces, one can succeed in creating a new unique expression of Energy, a new unique expression of Consciousness, or new unique expression of Oneness. To help you better understand how Consciousness is never destroyed or created and only ever changes from one form to another by combining it with other unique expressions of itself and subjecting it to external forces, I invite you to consider the water molecule, a universally present and unique expression of Consciousness.

A water molecule is made up of three unique expressions of Energy: two hydrogen atoms and one oxygen atom. By combining these three atoms, or individual expressions of Energy, Consciousness, or Oneness, you create a new expression of Energy, Consciousness, or Oneness, which we unanimously know as water. If you subject the water molecules to different forces, you can change its frequency of vibration so that it now expresses itself as either denser, or less dense, than before. This is similar to saying you change its physical expression. If the external force was cold air, another unique expression of Energy, the water molecules would vibrate slower, become thicker, and take on a solid shape, which we unanimously know as ice. On the other hand, if the external force you applied to the ice was hot air, another unique expression of Energy, the ice's frequency of vibration would increase. The ice would melt and then express itself as free-flowing water ready to take on the shape of any container. Adding more heat (hot air) to the water molecule would further increase its vibration. The water molecule would evaporate, become less dense than water, and turn into steam. As steam, the molecule would take up more volume, or space.

Now, it is essential for you to understand that at no point in time is the combination of two hydrogen atoms and one oxygen atom either separate from or not Consciousness, Oneness, or Energy. Please realize that regardless of the water molecule's frequency of vibration, it is always a part of Consciousness as its truest, basic, and most fundamental essence.

Solely due to how fast or slow the combination of both atoms are vibrating (dependent on the external forces), the atoms can express themselves as either ice, water, or steam. The state of the water molecule's physical expression has absolutely no effect on its purest and most fundamental essence. The water molecule is always, purely Consciousness, Oneness, or Energy.

This simple, yet profound, example applies to every other thing that exists throughout the cosmos. This is true. Every single thing that exists, in its purest form, is Energy, Consciousness, or Oneness vibrating at its very own unique frequency.

Every single thing you can see, touch, feel, hear, or smell, including your thoughts and other things you cannot perceive or are not aware of, are all unique expressions of Consciousness, Oneness, or Energy that are vibrating at differing and unique frequencies. The bread and food you eat, the air you are currently breathing, and the clothing you have on are all unique expressions of the same Consciousness, Oneness, or Energy. The trees in your favorite city park, the clouds in the sky, the volcanic mountains across our lovely planet, the furniture in your house, the car you drive, the doorknob on the door in your office, and the stones in your yard are no different. Neither are the oceans, the grass on the soccer fields, the seats on Boeing's most innovative planes, the building you live in, insects, birds, fish, nor lions in zoos or the wild. Every one of them is a unique expression of this same Consciousness, Oneness, or Energy vibrating at some unique frequency. A simple single hydrogen atom is an expression of this same vibrating Energy. A simple oxygen atom is also an expression of this same vibrating Energy.

Since you now understand the omnipresence of Consciousness as the basic and most fundamental essence of everything, it should make sense that you—the open-minded, brave soul reading this book right now—are, in your purest and most fundamental essence, also an individual expression of this same vibrating Energy with a unique frequency of vibration. This is correct. You are purely Consciousness. You are purely Oneness, and a very complex expression of it.

By examining your physical body, you can appreciate just how complex it is. Consider the many different unique expressions of Consciousness vibrating at different frequencies that come together to make up your body. I am referring to your internal organs, including your brain, lungs, heart, liver, gallbladder, kidneys, and pancreas. I am referring to parts of your body including your eyes, nose, teeth, tongue, tonsils, nerves, blood vessels, the hair on your head, your toes and fingers, your toenails and fingernails. I am referring to essential components of your body, including the bacteria in your gut and heart. As unique expressions of Consciousness themselves, your body parts and organs are all ceaselessly working with each other in their respective and essential roles to maintain your body in a homeostatic state and ensure your survival. For example, the bacteria in your gut, heart, and brain are unique expressions of Consciousness helping you, a more complex unique expression of Consciousness, make decisions, digest the food you eat, and prevent you from acquiring infections.

What It Means to Be Consciousness

To be Consciousness means to be omnipresent and to always exist. Consciousness reminds us of this essential aspect of what it means to be a unique expression of itself through myriad ways. Religious texts include examples of this universal truth. One such example is in the Bible, in the book of Exodus. In the story, Consciousness or Oneness directs Moses to tell the people of Israel that I AM sent him (Moses) to them (the Israelites) to deliver a message.

By Consciousness referring to itself as I AM, it not only signifies its omnipresence, but also that its presence is not subject to time as you and I currently perceive it. Essentially, Consciousness' omnipresence is timeless. Also, by referring to itself as I AM, Consciousness does not limit itself to any single label, description, or expression you can bestow on it. Consciousness is instead inviting you (or anyone, for that matter) to place any labels you wish at the end of the first two words, I AM, to describe it. Regardless of which name, noun, or adjective you choose, you would correctly describe who and what Consciousness is. You would further realize who and what I AM is, and how nothing that exists is separate from or outside of Consciousness.

Go ahead and give it a try if you wish. Complete the sentence, "I AM _____" to appreciate the omnipresence of Consciousness.

Simply put, Consciousness *is*. Whatever you can think of, in the moment that you think of it, means it already exists as a unique expression of Consciousness. Consciousness is everything, and everything is a unique expression of Consciousness.

Besides being omnipresent and always existing, you can appreciate this other essential aspect of what it means to be Consciousness as you build on your understanding of who you truly are. To be Consciousness also means every single thing that exists is an individual expression of itself, or of you. Though this might be a tough concept to grasp or accept as true, I need you to understand that it is, in fact, true.

If everything is a unique expression of itself, all of life's experiences encompass Consciousness in different forms, interacting with itself. This is an essential point for you to understand so, I will repeat it for you. All of life's experiences encompass Consciousness in different forms, interacting with itself. Or put another way, all of life's experiences are *You*, in different forms of *You*, interacting with yourself. This explains the connectedness of all things that I am sure you have heard of, either in your religious studies or through pop culture. The idea that God created everything in his image or that we are all one with the trees, animals, or stars in the sky, stems from this understanding.

After reading through Part II of this book, you will have a more in-depth understanding of why Consciousness behaves this way (interacts with itself). For now, trust that this is another essential quality of being Consciousness. In fact, this universal truth further supports the understanding that nothing exists outside of Consciousness, and instead that every single thing that exists originates from the same source: they all come from Consciousness.

You cannot speak or think of anything that is outside of Consciousness, as any such thing is unimaginable and indescribable. You might think that the absence of something is nothing, and therefore nothing is not Consciousness. That is an excellent thought to have; however, I invite you to consider the following explanation.

Understand that nothing is also Consciousness because nothing implies unoccupied space, and space allows something to exist by taking it up. You and everything you own and can see, for instance, would not exist without space. Because you exist, space exists, and vice versa. In other words, space is a unique expression of Consciousness, too. Truly, nothing that exists is separate from Consciousness.

Before there was unoccupied space, and something to take it up, there was 'no' thing. That means 'no' thing existed before Consciousness did. Even I cannot grasp the concept of 'no' thing, so I will not attempt to describe it any further.

In your spare time, I invite you to try imagining 'no' thing to experience how tough it is for yourself. Do not confuse 'no' thing with the idea of nothing or unoccupied space. 'No' thing is not Consciousness because 'no' thing does not currently exist, either in the physical realm or in thought. I, personally, cannot perceive 'no' thing.

You, on the other hand, exist, and are therefore an expression of Consciousness. Simply put, you *are* Consciousness. And you, as Consciousness, are not separate or different from everything else throughout the cosmos.

There is more to being Consciousness than being omnipresent and always existing, and interacting with unique expressions of itself. A third essential quality about being Consciousness, and probably the most important one, is this: as Consciousness, you are a co-creator of the entire universe and co-orchestrator of everything happening in it. This means that the entire universe is the way it is in this moment because of you and all other unique expressions of yourself currently incarnate here on Earth.

I can appreciate that you may find this idea hard to believe or even blasphemous, as you might hold the belief that a God created the universe and is orchestrating everything in it. There is absolutely nothing wrong with believing in a God that created everything, and therefore rendering yourself an inferior subject in the scenario. I believed the same thing for more than twenty-eight years of my life before remembering who and why we all were.

The notion of a God orchestrating everything in the universe is a beautiful, inaccurate, creative understanding of what is going on here, and there is a perfect explanation to why that is. I promise to explain why in Part II-A of this book. For now, I need you to understand that you are essentially the God you believe created the entire universe. As a god, you are co-creating the entire universe by creating, to a smaller scale, your own universe every day. This smaller scale universe is your current Earth life situation.

Everything about your current Earth life situation—including your friends, acquaintances, possessions, job, kids, stresses, and celebrations—is part of your life because you manifested them with your thoughts and beliefs, and because you are experiencing life on Earth, through your actions. No other person, unless you gave your power away, created the Earth life you are currently experiencing for yourself. If this still does not resonate with you, I can assure you that, after reading through Chapter 10, you will gain a more genuine appreciation and understanding of just how much power and influence you wield over the Earth life situation you create and experience for yourself.

Who You Think You Are

Now that you understand your truest and most fundamental form to be purely Consciousness, like all other things in the cosmos, and that as pure Consciousness, *You* can never cease to exist, I want to begin to clarify any confusion you have about the separate versions of yourself. By separate versions of yourself, I am referring to your finite self (your earthly self), and your infinite self (your purely Consciousness self).

Before I remembered and understood the differences, I believed that who I was, was entirely contained within my earthly self. Going forward, I refer to this aspect of me as my ego. I, or my ego, believed I was Roland Achenjang: a son, brother, cousin, pharmacist, and author obsessed with finding out who and why we all are. At the same time, I, or my ego, also believed I had a soul, but never fully understood much about my soul. I believed my soul existed in another realm—the spirit plane. I believed my soul was somehow separate from me but paradoxically still connected to me. I believed it was my duty, as Roland Achenjang, to live an earthly life that ensured that my soul would enjoy the experience of heaven after I, Roland Achenjang, died. I believed Roland Achenjang was finite, and my soul was infinite. Still, I wasn't sure where my soul came from.

You may believe the same things, or something similar, about yourself today. You, or your ego, believes that the you reading this book right now is a finite being moving closer to the end of its existence with every passing second. There is nothing wrong with holding onto this belief; however, I want to assure you of two things.

First, this earthly you is a unique expression of Consciousness; otherwise, it would not exist.

Second, and more importantly, this earthly you is an illusionary unique expression of Consciousness. It is not as real as you believe it to be. There is a perfectly beautiful reason for why that is, which I explain more in Chapter 5.

Earthly you, or your ego, is an illusionary expression of Consciousness, just like you believe the character in a video game or movie to be illusionary or not real. For example, I am sure you would consider the video game character Mario in Nintendo's Super Mario Brothers to be illusionary, or not as real, when compared to the you that is playing the game. Well, like you, Mario is also a unique expression of Consciousness and will always exist, albeit in a different form than you currently perceive. And second, like you, Mario is also an illusionary expression of Consciousness as you experience it from your current Earthly perspective—the perspective that makes you believe you are real, and that Mario is less real than you are.

Now, if the you reading this book, or your ego, is an illusionary version of *You* experiencing Earth life, you may wonder who the real you is. If you can recall what you read at the beginning of this chapter, the real *You* is an expression of the origin of every single thing that exists throughout the cosmos. The real you is your soul, the source from which your egoic self originates. *You* are pure Consciousness. *You* are an omnipresent, non-illusionary unique expression of Consciousness that will never cease to exist. All your Earthly experiences are the illusionary expression of *You,* your ego, interacting with other illusionary unique expressions of Consciousness. This non-illusionary expression of Consciousness, *You,* is who you truly are.

Going forward, I will continue to refer to the illusionary version of you experiencing life on Earth as your ego. To illustrate, Roland Achenjang, the author of this book, is my ego. When referencing your ego by using the word "you," I will keep the formatting simple, as in the following sentence: you think you are solely your ego. On the other hand, when you see the word *You* formatted as such, understand I am referring to the non-illusionary, ever-existing, and pure Consciousness you. I am referring to your soul.

Word Choice Matters

Before we go any further, I would like to take a minute to explain the beauty and limitations of words. People in different parts of the world use multiple words to describe their understanding of the all-encompassing Energy, this same entity I prefer to refer to as Oneness or Consciousness. People use words like God, Mother and Father God, Allah, God the Creator, or The Almighty Father.

I am sure you have come across other words in your lifetime that you have understood were referring to the creator of all things seen and unseen. To be clear, every one of these labels is likely referring to the same entity.

Consider that someone from Cameroon, like myself, grew up calling a specific, nutritious, unique expression of Consciousness a pear, while an American would refer to that same thing as an avocado. Neither of us would be wrong in this case, as labels used to describe any individual expression of Consciousness are often dependent on the environment or geographical location where they are found. That said, referring to this all-encompassing entity, Consciousness, with any one of the above names or something else you can think of is entirely appropriate.

As you will come to see in Part II of this book, however, I believe who or what most people refer to as God is a limited understanding and description of what Consciousness is. The idea of God creates a sense of inferiority for humans trying to understand the entity, and introduces a feeling of separation from the creator of all things. In addition to introducing these feelings, most people's idea of who and what God is severely limits what is limitless. That which every single thing that exists originates from is limitless and infinite.

I introduce this point to explain that throughout the rest of the book, I shall refer to this all-encompassing, limitless, and infinite omnipresent existence as Consciousness, Oneness, or Energy. Please begin to understand and appreciate that Consciousness transcends your understandings and beliefs of who or what God is.

If you can begin to accept and commit to understanding that the you reading this book is an illusionary unique expression of *You* or of Consciousness, you will facilitate your understanding of everything else about why you are, no matter how complex or elementary. Further, starting to appreciate this aspect of who you are will drastically improve your ability to experience Earth life in bliss. This is no fairy tale statement, but one of truth that is entirely possible for you. I write this because it is my current experience every day.

Never forget that in your purest and most fundamental essence, *You* are, always have been, and always will be pure Consciousness.

Recap of Who You Are

Every single thing that exists, whether living or dead, seen or unseen, originates from the same source. I refer to the source of all things as pure Consciousness, Energy, or Oneness.

Consciousness is timeless, omnipresent. It always exists, and always has existed.

Consciousness is infinite and limitless; it is Energy. Consciousness changes its form of existence by changing its frequency of vibration.

Regardless of how Consciousness expresses itself, it is never separate from or outside of being purely Consciousness as its purest form.

The entire universe is made up of Consciousness, as unique expressions of itself, interacting with itself.

All unique expressions of Consciousness are simultaneously co-creating the entire universe with their thoughts, words, and actions, or simply by being.

Your soul is a unique expression of Consciousness. It is *You*. *You* are the real you. *You* are pure Consciousness.

Your ego is a unique expression of Consciousness, though an illusionary unique expression of Consciousness, similar to how you perceive a video game character as not real.

Part II-A:

Why You Are (Your Earth Life Experience)

2

Why You Are

———————

"Shine like the universe is yours." —Rumi

To understand why you, the illusionary unique expression of *You*, are, first you need to remember and appreciate Consciousness. I explained in Chapter 1 that everything in existence throughout the cosmos is Consciousness interacting with unique expressions of itself to produce the experience. Consciousness does this because it is everything that exists. There is nothing that exists that isn't a unique expression of Consciousness, or of *You*. And because this is the case, all that unique expressions of *You* or of Consciousness have available to interact with is other unique expressions of *You* or of itself.

Imagine what you would do if you suddenly found yourself alone and isolated in a safe environment. As you imagine, make sure you understand that the environment is a safe one. In such an environment, after becoming aware of yourself, I imagine that you may begin to feel bored. To avoid feeling bored, you would come up with creative activities to entertain yourself. Kids under the age of seven are super adept at this skill. With a simple empty cardboard box, kids can create the most elaborate scenes and experiences for themselves. This is a very important characteristic of being Consciousness, and one of the most important reasons for why you are.

You Exist to Create

This is true. *You*, as Consciousness, have an insatiable desire to exist or experience life in an infinite array of forms or expressions. Consciousness satisfies this desire by creating new forms of itself, or new forms of existence ceaselessly. The more Consciousness becomes aware of itself, the more it is able to create new forms of existence of itself. Every created existence is temporary, and soon after Consciousness realizes that the existence provides it no more value, it ceases to exist in that form and changes into another. Often, the new form is more complex than the previous one. This is one reason why you exist. You exist to create increasingly complex, unique expressions of yourself, which becomes easier and easier the more you know or become aware of yourself.

Consider your existence for a minute. You exist because you are, first, a created form of existence of Consciousness. Just like all other forms of existence of Consciousness here on Earth, you are a temporary existence. Being temporary is another reason why you are an illusionary form of Consciousness. Besides being temporary, I also explained in the previous chapter that you are a very complex unique expression of Consciousness, given that many unique expressions of you make up who you are. In other words, you are an ever-evolving illusionary, unique expression of Consciousness.

Now, as a unique form of Consciousness, you also have a ceaseless desire to create. This is another reason why you are co-creator of the entire universal experience. Being a co-creator makes sense, because that which created you did so in its image. You, therefore, have similar characteristics. Think about your kids or your parents to appreciate what it means to have similar characteristics to that from which you originate.

Look around you right now to see the infinite unique expressions of you that you or some other unique expression of you has created. You can appreciate how endless and ever more increasingly complex the creations are. Take this book you are reading as an example. As the author of this book, realize that I am a unique expression of you that created it by collaborating with other unique expressions of you. Appreciate how complex the book is. Chapters in this book are made up of sub-sections, which are made up of paragraphs, which are made up of sentences, which are made up of words, which in turn, are made up of letters. The letters, words, sentences, paragraphs, sub-sections, and chapters are all unique expressions of Consciousness. Realize how the book, which encompasses all of it, is basically a complex existence of individual letters of the English alphabet.

The analysis above doesn't consider the pages in this book nor the cover and the cover design. It does not break down the elaborate printing mechanisms or the complex distribution networks in place to get the book to you in paperback or electronic form. If you take the time to consider those aspects of this book's existence, you can begin to appreciate how complex they are. By being that way, they are exhibiting characteristics of being Consciousness — existing in myriad forms that are increasingly complex.

Examine any other piece of creation, such as your house, television, car, or cell phone. They are all unique expressions of you that you, or some other unique expression of you, created. Appreciate how, over time, each one of them has become increasingly complex. Take the cell phone: it is a wonderful example of Consciousness' desire to exist in an infinite array of forms that become increasingly complex, and to cease to exist in a particular form once the form provides itself (Consciousness) no more value. Ceasing to exist in a particular form implies that, that form transforms into a different form, which provides itself (Consciousness) more value or a more complex way to exist. Think of the phones that are no longer in production, like the 1987 Nokia Cityman. When Consciousness learned of a more complex way to exist that provided itself more value, it transformed from the 1987 Nokia Cityman to the 2018 Nokia 8110, or the even more complex Nokia 9 PureView. So, yes, as an illusionary, unique expression of Consciousness, you exist to help Consciousness fulfill its ceaseless desire to create increasingly complex expressions of itself. That, however, is not the whole story. There is another reason for why you are.

You Exist to Experience Emotions

Again, this is true, and it complements the reason you exist to create. Your creations, regardless of what they are, are all excellent avenues for you to express and experience a wide array of emotions and feelings. You can use your thoughts, words, or actions to express or experience any emotions you desire. You could draw a picture, make a painting, dance, sing, write, or act in any manner of your choosing that helps you express or experience an emotion.

Like Consciousness' ceaseless desire to exist in an infinite array of forms, it also has a ceaseless desire to express and experience an infinite array of emotions. Throughout the cosmos, unique expressions of Consciousness are expressing and experiencing emotions that we on Earth will never experience and cannot even fathom. Earthly emotions available for you to experience range from deathly fear to heavenly joy. Not to be outdone, however, we have a wide range of emotions that we can experience here on Earth that other beings may never experience and probably cannot fathom, either. The character

Spark in the popular series *Star Trek* is an excellent example of a being from another planet who is incapable of experiencing emotions that human beings can.

Like your creations, your emotions are also temporary, illusionary experiences that you seek to augment as soon as they cease to provide you any value. By augment, I mean you seek to experience them in increasingly complex ways or in increasing magnitudes. This should come as no surprise to you because it is a fundamental characteristic of being Consciousness.

You are now aware of two reasons why Consciousness exists. One reason is to experience life in an infinite array of forms, and the other is to experience an infinite array of emotions. You may be wondering about the purpose for doing this. Put another way, what value is there in existing in temporary (creating and changing), ever more complex forms and experiencing temporary, ever more complex emotions? This brings me to the third reason for your existence.

Providing Value to Consciousness

Consciousness exists in the balance of creating and changing because these two simple activities provide it infinite opportunities to continuously learn about and get to know itself. Ceaselessly creating and changing helps Consciousness improve its understanding of itself and its infinite capabilities. Both activities support Consciousness' ceaseless growth and acquisition of knowledge. Both activities allow Consciousness to expand its consciousness.

Recall that Consciousness is everything—meaning, it is all it has, to interact with. As Consciousness continues to interact with itself, it becomes more aware of its existence. Becoming more self-aware teaches Consciousness of its infinitely creative capabilities. Consciousness, therefore, naturally leverages its latest understanding of its infinitely creative abilities to continue to create and change its existence. This is what has been happening since the beginning of time. And since you now understand that Consciousness' existence will never cease, you can begin to appreciate that neither will its desires to expand knowledge of itself.

Think of every created manifestation that you are currently aware of or can experience with any of your five senses and your thoughts. Appreciate that all of them are a unique expression of the same Consciousness from which you originate. Now, revel in the fact that every one of the manifestations currently experiencing life on Earth is a temporary experience or existence designed to help Consciousness expand knowledge of itself. Put another way, every experience or existence is providing Consciousness information about who it is, what it is, the myriad ways in which it can experience existence and emotions, and the infinite ways in which it can express itself. This is the basis of the knowledge that God is all-knowing. Well, not God, but Consciousness is all knowing.

Consciousness is a repository of every single existence, experience, action, thought, or word that all unique expressions of itself have partaken in, since it started becoming aware of itself—since the beginning of time. This is true, and it explains a great deal of why you exist. Simply put, you exist to expand your consciousness, which simultaneously expands *Your* consciousness, and inevitably expands Consciousness' consciousness. By consciousness, I mean knowledge of yourself and your infinite ability to create. Every single thing you or any other unique expression of Consciousness does, at all times, supports this very same outcome. They all provide information that supports Consciousness' ability to learn and teach itself about itself. If you are confused about what you just read, this would be a good time to pause and re-read this section. If you feel confident that you are beginning to understand your role in the cosmos, then by all means, proceed.

I appreciate that you are now aware of why you are, but may still be confused about why Earth life is the way it is—you know, providing you with vast opportunities to perceive experiences of suffering, pain, and fears. As you will come to see in Chapters 3 and 4, the entire Earth life experience is as it is to help Consciousness learn more about itself; however, just as there are other areas throughout the cosmos where Consciousness exists and accomplishes this same goal, the Earth life experience has a set of rules, forces, and aspects that render the experience different and unique. If this confuses you, think of video games to help you understand the point:

Creators of video games have a set of rules, limitations, and designs that allow players of the game to experience emotions or learnings in the way they (the creators) intended. For instance, the rules and design of the video game Super Mario Brothers, played on Nintendo consoles, are unique to that game. So are the rules and design of the video game Halo, played on Microsoft's Xbox consoles. As the creators intended, you cannot play Super Mario Brothers as Halo's Master Chief. This is no different for all unique expressions of Consciousness experiencing life on Earth. You and I are equally subject to certain rules, which I delve into in the next chapter.

Recap of Why You Are

Consciousness has an insatiable desire to experience life expressed in an infinite array of forms. You are one such form of expressions, and it is one reason why you are.

Consciousness has an insatiable desire to experience an infinite array of emotions. You help Consciousness do just that in all that you think, say, and do.

Your existence and experiences provide Consciousness with an infinite amount of information to continue to become self-aware, to grow, and to expand knowledge of itself.

Like video game universes, Earth has specific rules and design elements that render its experience what it is for you. I expand on these rules and elements in the next two chapters.

3

Two Rules Govern
Your Earth Life Experience

―――――――

"At the end of the day, you are your own lawmaker."
―Bangambiki Habyarimana

B uilding on the knowledge that your life on Earth is intended to help Consciousness expand knowledge of itself, I think it is important that you understand the two rules governing the experience. These two rules equally affect everything you do, and everything and everyone on Earth. Both rules have no exceptions. To build on your understanding of why you are and why your Earthly experience is what it is, you must become familiar with these rules and understand what they are.

As a word of caution, I want you to appreciate that it is easy to get them confused with what they are not. I am confident you have come across these rules at some point in your life, but you may not have been aware of what they meant or how they applied to you, so you misunderstood them. That is fine. I am also confident and hopeful that the explanations I provide will rectify this issue for you once and for all.

As of this instance, understanding what the rules are is necessary for you, as it will have a tremendous impact on you accepting the universal truths I present in this book, and subsequently knowing, or better yet, remembering why you are. Not only that, it will improve your ability to find peace and bliss in your life regardless of its current state or situation. I say this will help you *know* or *remember* why you are because right now you are only *aware* of why you are after reading the previous chapter. *Knowing* comes from experience – the experience could be remembering through meditating, as was my case. And until you remember this information, you are unfortunately limited to only being *aware* of the information.

The Rules

Rule One: For every action, there is an equal and opposite reaction.

If you recall from the first chapter, everything, including you, is a unique expression of Consciousness. You can only change unique expressions of this Consciousness from one form to another and can never destroy it. Also, everything that exists is an individual manifestation of itself. That said, all of Consciousness is subject to the rule of action and equal and opposite reaction. That is to say, the outcome of every action of a defined magnitude any unique expression of Consciousness takes will result in the experience of an opposite reaction of equal magnitude by another unique expression of Consciousness. In other words, Consciousness always returns to a state of balance throughout its existence in the universe, including on Earth. Nothing and no one can permanently disturb this balance.

To help you understand this rule and its effects on Earth, consider a form of Consciousness expressing itself as wind, and its impact on another form of Consciousness expressing itself as a piece of cloth—let's call it a flag. On a beautiful summer day, if the wind acts by moving across a flag, the flag will react by moving or flapping in a wave-like pattern. The flapping of the flag is the reaction to the action of the wind moving across it, and the vigorousness at which the flag flaps is dependent on the speed of the wind that moved across it as well. If this example fails to demonstrate how simple and uncomplicated the rule is to you, I invite you to consider another example.

Imagine a form of Oneness expressed as the Sun's rays (heat source), and its effects on another form of Oneness expressed as water. If the Sun's rays act on the water molecules, the water molecules react by evaporating into water vapor and rising into the atmosphere. As the water vapor rises, colder air higher up in the atmosphere acts on the water molecules, and the water molecules react by condensing back to water until they are heavy enough to fall back down to Earth as rain. The speed at which the water molecules evaporate into water vapor is dependent on how hot the sun's rays are, and, likewise, the rate at which the water vapor condenses is dependent on how cold the air in the atmosphere is. If the air is frigid, the water vapor condenses into a solid shape and falls back to Earth as either hail or snow.

Bringing the understanding of rule number one closer to home, realize that your body, as a micro-cosmic expression of Consciousness, is always attempting to maintain itself in homeostasis. Your body possess intrinsic feedback mechanisms designed to do just that. If your cells need water, biologic process in your body tell you brain you are thirsty. You then act to balance the feeling of being thirsty by drinking. If you end up drinking a lot of water, your body's cells and organs will absorb as much of the water as they need and then get rid of the rest, either through perspiration or urination. The same thing happens after you eat, pursuant to a signal that you are hungry. Your body will absorb all the nutrients and energy it needs from the food, and then excrete the rest.

In unfortunate circumstances when your body is out of balance for an extended period, you might end up experiencing any one of the myriad diseases you can think of. This state of being out of balance also needs to be balanced. You work to return the balance by seeking medical advice and possibly taking pharmaceuticals. Realize that the medical community exists as a reaction to the action that left you feeling out of balance. The medical community is also a unique expression of Consciousness working to return all of Consciousness back to balance—back to a state of homeostasis. And through its work, it is helping Consciousness expand its consciousness.

It is essential that you understand precisely what rule number one declares and not confuse it with something else. The idea of opposite has no relation to an experience being good or bad. *Opposite* simply means a counterbalancing reaction to the action that has occurred. I need you to be cognizant of the fact that the rule does not state that for every *good* action of an absolute magnitude there will be a *bad* reaction of equal magnitude. This is precisely not what the rule states, and thinking in this manner is incorrect, as you will come to see in Chapter 7. Thinking in this manner will also significantly hinder your ability to continue to build on your understanding of why you are.

Nothing about the rule supports the belief that if you do something good of an absolute magnitude, you will then experience something good of equal magnitude. Neither does the rule support the notion that if you do something good of an absolute magnitude, you or some other unique expression of Consciousness will then experience something bad of the same magnitude. Both beliefs are not what the rule declares, and I implore you not to confuse the two. If you have always thought that was the case and are serious about learning the universal truths about why you are, I implore you to change your views on the matter before proceeding. If you need to take a week to accept this, that is absolutely fine. Put the book down, and come back to it when you are ready to proceed.

The rule is straightforward and strictly declares that for every action, there is an equal and opposite reaction. That is it. No need to complicate it.

Rule Two: Consciousness is loved unconditionally and has free will.

Rule number two is more natural to explain and understand, but I appreciate that it might be a more difficult rule to accept as true. As written, the rule bestows upon you and every unique expression of Consciousness full authority to decide and partake in any imaginative or creative experiences it wishes to have while on Earth. Even more important, the rule bestows unconditional love upon you and all unique expressions of Consciousness.

You may wonder who has the authority to bestow unconditional love to every single thing that exists, and the answer is that Consciousness does; *You* do. This is another universal truth that I need you to accept going forward. Consciousness, meaning every single thing that exists, loves you and every single thing that exists, unconditionally. I deliberately chose not to say God loves you unconditionally in this case because, as I have already stated, your idea of God is subjective and limited by your beliefs and Earth life experiences. Consciousness, on the other hand, encompasses everything that *is* and transcends your ideas of God. Believe it or not, the God you believe in is an illusionary, unique expression of Consciousness.

Anyway, as the rule is written, the collective unique expressions of Consciousness, including you, bestow upon all unique expressions of Consciousness, including you, unconditional love.

The idea of unconditional love is not complicated, though again, you might want to complicate it. Unconditional love simply means love that is without conditions. There is no need for you to confuse the statement or its understanding, and I implore you not to continue to confuse it with something else, beginning in this instant and for the rest of your life.

I do appreciate that it might be hard to understand this rule. You may not be able to accept it for yourself because of your beliefs of being inferior to your creator. You might still believe that you are not capable of saving yourself and need someone to save you from your wrongdoings. I held on to similar beliefs in the past, but since August 21st, 2018, I have known that this is not the case. Unconditional love means you are loved despite your actions. It means you are loved simply for existing or being, whether as a real or illusionary unique expression of Consciousness.

I also appreciate that this rule might be hard to understand because you may think you are not able to provide unconditional love to another unique expression of Consciousness. That is a perfectly normal belief to hold, though it is a false belief. As a unique expression of Consciousness, you already do love unconditionally and just do not remember. Your inability to remember reflects your current level of awareness of your connection to Consciousness. That said, I must applaud you for reading this book because it demonstrates your willingness to work towards remembering.

In addition to loving you unconditionally, rule number two also states that Consciousness grants you and all other unique expressions of itself free will to do as you please at any moment of your life while on Earth. This means you can think anything, say whatever you like, and act in any manner of your choosing, at any time of your choosing. Because Consciousness loves you unconditionally and grants you free will to do as you please, it does not matter what you choose to do, how you decide to do it, when you decide to do it, how often you choose to do it, and with whom you want to do it. Regardless of what you do, you must start believing and accepting that Consciousness grants you all the rights and full authority to do it.

I promise you that Consciousness will love you unconditionally, forever, either way. This is a universal truth, and I implore you not to complicate this truth or try to make it into what it is not.

So, Why Have Both Rules?

Think about it. Consciousness is present throughout the cosmos, and on Earth, as unique expressions of itself. Consciousness has an insatiable desire to exist in infinite forms, and to express and experience an infinite array of emotions. Consciousness also has an insatiable desire to continue to expand knowledge of itself. Consciousness understands that it can most effectively achieve this by creating multiple illusionary versions of itself to exist, create, and express themselves simultaneously, without hindrance, through different experiences and worlds.

For this to happen in perpetuity, the two rules must exist as they do. If the balance is not maintained, Consciousness will cease to exist as it does. I cannot fathom how, or in what fashion, Consciousness would exist if it did not maintain this balance, and frankly I do not think it is necessary to try to fathom how. It is like imaging *'no' thing*, which I have already pointed out to you as unfathomable.

Second, if you are not loved unconditionally and granted free will, your ability to help Consciousness most effectively learn about itself will be severely limited. Consciousness does not want this for itself, and I understand why. Matter of fact, so should you. It would be limiting and inefficient. Frankly, you would not want the same for yourself, if put in the same position. Who am I kidding—you *are* in the same situation, and that is why you already love unconditionally and grant free will to all unique expressions of yourself.

To appreciate just how powerful these two rules are, think about what you would do if there were no consequences for your actions, except the consequence of infinitely growing in understanding of who and why you are. This is essentially the perspective from which Consciousness operates. If everything you do is helping Consciousness expand knowledge of itself, why wouldn't it love you unconditionally for it and grant you free will to do as you please? This question is an important one to consider, particularly because Consciousness is all that is, and nothing and no one can harm it.

Rules One and Two in Perspective

Never forget that rules one and two govern every single action that presents itself as the illusion of real that you experience here on Earth. Also, know that every experience you take part in and every action that you undertake are both dependent on your rights to free will. This means that you have full power, authority, and responsibility to choose your perceptions of any of your experiences, along with how you act in the moment of the experiences.

Additionally, by examining both rules, you will appreciate how they declare that, regardless of the action you take, what will result is an equal and opposite reaction of the same magnitude. This means some unique expression of Consciousness somewhere will experience the opposite reaction of equal magnitude. The unique expression of Consciousness experiencing the opposite reaction could be you as well.

Rules number one and two never fail, and they do not have preferences or exceptions. They equally affect every unique expression of Consciousness here on Earth. This is an excellent time to remind you that rule number one, the rule of equal and opposite reactions, does not support any beliefs of being right or wrong. Nowhere does it state that benevolent deeds of a certain magnitude will result in benevolent deeds of the same magnitude, and/or vice versa. Lastly, understand how both rules declare that, regardless of what actions you take and their resulting reactions, Consciousness will always love you unconditionally.

I cannot stress enough the importance of understanding both rules and what they declare, and the need for you not to confuse them with what they do not declare. Both rules are simple. Do not complicate them.

Recap of Rules Governing Your Earth Life Experience

Two rules equally govern all of Consciousness experiencing life throughout the cosmos. They equally apply to all unique expressions of Consciousness currently experiencing life on Earth.

Rule one states simply that every action will result in an equal and opposite reaction. The rule declares that Consciousness always returns to a state of balance.

Rule two states simply that every unique expression of Consciousness is loved unconditionally and has free will. Essentially, this rule declares that Consciousness loves itself. This is possible because there is nothing outside of Consciousness.

4

Unique Aspects Distort
Your Earth Life Perceptions

"The ego says, I shouldn't have to suffer, and that thought makes you suffer so much more." —Eckhart Tolle

E very second you spend on Earth validates your bravery. You continue to fight for your survival only because you do not remember that you have no end.

I do appreciate that the two rules discussed in the previous chapter can be hard to accept as true because, while on Earth, certain unique aspects distort the realities of the rules. And by so doing, these unique aspects affect how you perceive yourself and your earthly experiences.

To continue to build on your understanding of why you are, you must also become aware of and familiar with these unique aspects. Work to understand them, because, once you do, including how they affect your Earth life experiences, I promise it will enhance your ability to remember who and why you are. Additionally, understanding these unique aspects will help you find and experience joy and bliss in your earthly experiences. I truly believe it is necessary to recognize how vital these unique aspects are, and the contributions they make towards your illusionary Earth life experiences.

I also do not believe these same aspects are part of the experiences for other unique expressions of Consciousness living in different parts of the universe. What I mean by that is, they are unique to experiencing life solely on Earth. They are part of the Earth life design. They are the allure that attracts many brave souls, like you and me, to incarnate on Earth. If you chose to incarnate in another part of the universe, then the unique design aspects of that experience would vary from Earth's. They might have some similarities, but I have a hard time believing they would be the same. I say this because repeating the same experiences in another universe is an inefficient way for Consciousness to expand its knowledge. I am sure you can appreciate this notion. There is no need to duplicate experiences or efforts.

That said, I'll get right to explaining why your perception of life on Earth might not always be blissful or peaceful; why you perceive and believe the illusions of suffering, pain, anger, death, and fear. There are three simple reasons for this, and again, these reasons are unique to life on Earth, as far as I know. Below are the three unique aspects that render your experience of life on Earth what it is.

Unique Aspect One: Abandonment

I kid you not when I tell you that to fully and wholeheartedly understand why you are, you must appreciate the importance of this unique earthly aspect. I refer to it as abandonment. I am confident you will gain the most value out of this book by understanding abandonment and its role in your Earth life experience. Additionally, you will attain your greatest personal growth by understanding how abandonment has affected your life. Believe me, this universal truth is why you paid for this book or why someone who loves you bought it for you. Please pay it serious attention and come back to read this section over and over until you are blue in the face, or until you remember that it is, indeed, true. Once you remember the illusion of abandonment, I promise you the rest of your life will never be the same. Even if you do not remember, just being aware of it should help you to begin to understand it. Once you fully understand it, it will help to build on your understanding of the fact the life on Earth is not really what you have come to believe it to be.

Although all unique expressions of Consciousness are eternally connected by their purest and most fundamental essence, a requirement to incarnate and partake in the Earth life experience is to forget the existence of this eternal connection. This is a universal truth, and it is important for you to never forget this. All unique expressions of Consciousness experiencing life on Earth must temporarily forget the existence of their eternal connectedness to Consciousness. Everyone partaking in the Earth life experience must go through this experience early in their childhood. It could happen while you are in your mother's womb, but it most often happens by the time you are seven years old.

Everyone must forget who they are in their purest and most fundamental essence. Everyone, including you and me, must experience this. We all must forget about our eternal connection to Consciousness if we are to fully partake in the Earth life experience. This is a requirement that no one can bypass. There are no exceptions.

Returning to the analogy of Earth life being similar to a video game, think of the notion of playing Super Mario Brothers as Master Chief from Halo. We can both agree that in their current design, you cannot do that. This was not the intention of the creators of Super Mario Brothers. Neither can you, as Mario, defeat King Koopa in Super Mario Brothers using Master Chief's weapons. Employing this same understanding, please, please, please understand the current design of the Earth life experience requires that all participants forget their eternal connection to Consciousness. You cannot *play* the Earth life game if you do not agree to undergo this experience (abandonment), or if you do not agree to play by its designed rules.

After forgetting your eternal connection to Consciousness, or after forgetting that you are truly *You*, you are left with a feeling of desertion, neglect, or abandonment. You will feel lost and lonely. Since this feeling renders you incapable of remembering your eternal connection to Consciousness, it introduces a new type of emotion for you to experience. You know this emotion all too well. It is the driving force of all your earthly experiences. It is the emotion of fear. Even though fear is only an illusion, you start to believe it because you do not remember your eternal connection to Consciousness. You start to believe the fear that you are truly abandoned. Over time, the feelings, emotions, and experiences of fear continue to grow and cause you to become primarily focused on protecting yourself. This is a perfectly logical behavior to adopt given the circumstances. I mean, what else are you to do if you feel abandoned, rejected, neglected, and alone? Worst of all, what are you to do if you begin to experience fear?

Every unique expression of Consciousness experiencing life on Earth that currently does not remember their eternal connection to Consciousness is living under the illusion that they are alone and have to protect themselves. Since you now are aware that the belief of Consciousness abandoning you is an illusion, you can begin to appreciate that you Earth life experiences and perceptions, though they might seem real, are all an illusion too.

Further, you can begin to appreciate that all the fears you experience while on Earth, and in the myriad forms and ways you perceive them, are also illusions. They all stem from the false fear that Consciousness has abandoned you. They all stem from the false fear of not remembering who you are in your purest and most fundamental essence. They all stem from not remembering that you are also an illusion having a temporary experience on Earth. They all stem from not remembering that *You* always have been, are, and always will be, Consciousness. I expand more on the knowledge that Earth life is an illusion in Chapter 5.

Returning to the false belief of abandonment, you need to understand that the outcome of not remembering your eternal connection is that you spend your Earth life experience protecting yourself from illusionary fears that you believe will harm you. This is true. The illusion of abandonment is the genesis of all earthly perceptions of fear, pain, suffering, struggles, sadness, hell, and every awful thing you can think of.

If you examine all your beliefs and current life situation, you will start to notice how you created the beliefs because of a need to protect yourself from some fear that resonated with you. You created the beliefs to ensure your survival because you believe you are all that you are. Knowing this makes it easier to understand how the perceptions of Earth life experiences will all arise from a fear-based and need-to-survive feeling for any unique expression of Consciousness that does not remember their eternal connection to Consciousness.

Know that not remembering your eternal connection to Consciousness does not mean it does not exist. Your eternal connection is as strong as it has ever been, and no one severed it. The link has been and is always there. Understand that you needed to forget its existence in order to fully experience the illusions of fear while experiencing life on Earth. This temporary and illusionary belief is a necessary component of the grand illusion that is the Earth life experience. Besides, agreeing to incarnate on Earth meant accepting to forget your eternal connection, which is additional testament to just how brave of a soul you are. To make great strides in remembering why you are, you must become conscious of the fact that every single fear you possess stems from your illusionary belief that Consciousness has abandoned you here on Earth to fend for yourself.

Besides the illusion of abandonment, there is another unique aspect affecting your earthly perceptions. The second unique aspect is a component of *You*. You know this unique aspect better than anyone else in the world. In fact, I introduced this part of you in Chapter 1.

Unique Aspect Two: The Illusionary *You*—Your Ego

Since the feeling of abandonment causes you to forget your purest state of being and your eternal connection to Consciousness, you are left with no choice but to come up with a new understanding of who you are. The understanding, however, is an understanding of the illusionary *You*—a pseudo version of yourself. Appreciate how this new, illusionary *You* is based entirely on a lie because its entire existence originates from a state of fear and inaccurate beliefs. It originates from being aware of yourself after experiencing the illusion of abandonment, and the inaccurate belief that Consciousness has abandoned you to fend for yourself. This new, alternate persona is what I introduced to you as your ego in Chapter 1. Similar to how essential it is for you to have a physical body in order to fully experience Earth life, it is just as essential for you to develop an ego to ensure your survival on Earth, especially after you forget your eternal connection to Consciousness.

Your ego is primarily who you identify with as you experience life on Earth. Your ego is who you identify with as you continue to live under the illusionary fear that Consciousness has abandoned you to fend for yourself. Everything you believe and accept as true that someone close to you can use to describe your beliefs, habits, and behavior, are constructs of your ego. Your current life situation, or the life circumstances you find yourself in, are also a result of overcoming fear-based beliefs created by your ego. Your ego compels you to subscribe to morals, norms, traditions, and beliefs you believe will continue to protect you as you experience Earth life.

Your ego is the genesis of everything you believe. It accurately portrays who you think you are and how you would love the world to perceive you. Your ego also develops earthly desires, wishes, and dreams that you work so hard to attain but can never truly satisfy. Your ego, because of fear, creates a duality spectrum to help you identify and categorize experiences as either pleasant or unpleasant. Your ego, in trying to understand the universe, created academic studies like the studies of mathematics and science. Your ego also came up with creative explanations for why things are, including your current ideas of God and Satan. It is easy to see how your ego might even perceive itself as inferior, by employing its limited understandings of the workings of the universe as it tries to understand its creator.

Your ego is all I have described above, and much more. If you take nothing else from all I wrote, please recognize how necessary your ego is for you to be able to survive and continue to take part in Earth life experiences. You may think of your ego as an avatar, or a character in a video game. For instance, the character, Mario allows you to play the game Super Mario Brothers. In my case, my ego, Roland Achenjang, allows the real me, my soul, to play the Earth life game. Without my ego, my soul would not be able to partake in the Earth life experience.

Another universal truth I would love to share is this: because your ego is experiencing life on Earth, even as an illusion, it is subject to both rules governing all of Earth life discussed in the previous chapter. This means, regardless of the thoughts, believes and actions of your ego, Consciousness will continue to love your ego unconditionally. You can appreciate why that is by realizing that everything your ego does is helping Consciousness continue to expand knowledge of itself. Besides, through all of its experiences, your ego is moving closer to remembering that its existence is entirely an illusion, and also that the real you is pure Consciousness. When you finally remember this universal truth about who you truly are and stop identifying with your ego, some very interesting things happen. First, you recognize that all your fears are illusions and can be quickly overcome. Second, you accept that there is no need to continue living under the belief that you are separate from Consciousness, and you start to embody your pure self. When this happens, your ego proceeds to die (a form of change).

A Little Bit about Ego Death

The process of your ego dying is often referred to as ego death. Really, the experience is a change in your frequency of vibration from lower, fear-based vibrations to higher, unconditional-love-based vibrations. These changes signify a gravitation away from fear and towards bliss. Ego death occurs at a point in your life after you remember your eternal connection to Consciousness, which initiates the beginning of the end of all the fear-based beliefs your ego created. You begin to let go of all the beliefs you held on to that caused you to create a safe environment around the illusionary, separated, and abandoned you.

Ego death is a beautiful experience, though it is not without hardships. My experience with the process continues to be varied, but always interesting. I'll share one example of this with you.

For a long time, I kept having the same recurring dreams in which I came close to experiencing death. The experience of death in my dreams came to me in myriad forms. In one dream, I was a passenger on an airliner about to crash. In another instance, an armed robber broke through my front door and met me in my kitchen. He held his right arm up at shoulder level with a revolver in his hand. He pointed it at my forehead and was ready to pull the trigger. The scenes and experiences varied, but the experience of death was constant. Many times, in fear, I woke up before I could die. Funny enough, I would regret that I woke up because it was only a dream. My ego wasn't really going to die. When I was brave enough to stare death in the face in my dreams, the scenes would change to something beautiful and serene, and I would never really die in my dreams.

In the plane crash dream for instance, I recall becoming aware of my fate and accepting it. I remember sitting upright in my chair, confirming that my seatbelt was fastened, and then taking a deep breath. The rough weather we were flying through jolted the airliner in multiple directions, causing it to nose-dive. The pilots struggled to control the plane and made frequent announcements over the intercom alerting passengers to brace for a hard landing. I remained calm. Through all the turbulence and excitement, the plane came closer and closer to hitting the ground. Seconds before impact, the scene changed, and the plane landed safely on the runway. No one was hurt.

Because of frequent dreams like that, and because of my addiction to meditating, my perceptions of my Earth life experience have transformed significantly. I have overcome many of my fears. In fact, I often become aware of not being fearful of people, things, or experiences that once scared me only after experiencing them without fear. It is an odd feeling, though I have gotten used to it and actually enjoy it. Imagine knowing that you were once afraid of an experience and then remembering that fear while fearlessly partaking in the experience. In the moment, you might think, *Should I be worried about this like I always have been?* but you will realize you do not have the capacity to worry. It truly is an odd feeling. When I realize a fear I have overcome, I often smile and feel joy in my heart.

Back to discussing ego death. You can imagine the difficulties that arise as you shed years of your personality, beliefs, and the only world you have come to know. It is additionally scary because the future, which is life as a new person, is often uncertain. It is as though you are reborn as an adult, needing to learn survival skills all over again. Take refuge in knowing that losing this illusionary identity of yourself paves way for the real, infinitely creative, and purely Consciousness you to emerge. This new you will eventually find the process of learning and assimilating into Earth life to be a blissful experience.

Living from the real you's perspective, no longer will your desires and beliefs come from a space of fear of abandonment. You will create from a space of knowing who you are in your most fundamental essence. You will create from a space of possibility. As someone currently experiencing such a transformation, I consider this to be a tremendous blessing. I am quickly learning it is best not to resist the changes as I encounter them, like the opportunities to die in my dreams.

Mainstream information may have led you to believe that your ego is an awful part of your being that must be destroyed. This is true to an extent, as ego death introduces you to your real, authentic self. As I have previously stated, however, your ego is a necessity if you intend on experiencing Earth life.

Remember, it was your conscious decision to incarnate on Earth because Earth offers the opportunity to experience life under the illusion that you are separate from Consciousness. Your ego is what helps keep you safe as you continue to experience and believe the feeling and circumstances of abandonment. Your ego is also infinitely creative, as evidenced by your beliefs and current understandings of what is going on here on Earth, and of who or what the creator of the whole experience is. There is another important thing your ego does, for you, to continue to ensure your survival on Earth. I discuss this next.

Unique Aspect Three: Duality

I will refer to the third unique aspect contributing to how you perceive your experiences of the illusion that is life on Earth as, duality. Like the first two aspects, I need you to also pay special attention to duality.

As a quick recap, you are now aware that abandonment causes you to create and identify with a pseudo persona known as your ego. You also are aware that an essential role of your ego is to ensure your survival. Your ego ensures your survival by using your created beliefs to assist you in categorizing your Earth life experiences as either pleasant or unpleasant and good or evil, or, in other words, contraries.

This belief in Earth life experiences being separate from and contrary to each other is duality. Duality is the unique aspect of Earth life that allows you to categorize your experiences anywhere on a spectrum of what you would consider favorable or unfavorable; good or evil. I will refer to this spectrum going forward as your duality spectrum.

Your duality spectrum is entirely subjective and unique to you and you alone. The spectrum has two ends representing contraries. One end of the spectrum includes experiences you would categorize as so pleasant and enjoyable that you would consider them as similar to experiencing your idea of God/heaven. These are experiences and feelings that make you feel safe and connected, and your ego seeks to experience them repeatedly. The other end of the spectrum includes experiences you would categorize as the entire contrary, meaning the most unpleasant and disgusting feelings and experiences you want nothing to do with. You would consider these experiences as similar to experiencing your subjective understandings of Satan/hell.

Again, your duality spectrum is entirely subjective and unique to just you. Where you place your Earth life experiences on your spectrum between heaven and hell is dependent on many factors, and they change as your awareness of yourself changes. For example, your current Earth life situation—meaning your current health status, social circle, job, and work responsibilities—influences how you rate your earthly experiences. If your overall life situation is pleasant, you are likely going to rate your experiences as being somewhere on the heavenly side of your spectrum. If your current life situation changes and becomes unpleasant, say you are fired from your job or you get a divorce, you are likely to rate your experiences as being on the hellish side of your spectrum.

Your norms, morals, traditions, and beliefs are all influenced by the environment and community that you grew up in, and the fears that you experienced while growing up. They, too, will influence how you rate your experiences on your duality spectrum. If you move to another country and begin to adopt a new set of norms, morals, and traditions, notice how this too will cause you to change how your rate your experiences on your spectrum. Your beliefs are particularly important in influencing how you rate your experiences. I dedicate Chapter 9 to discussing the power of your beliefs and their effects on your Earth life experiences. For now, I need you to be aware that your beliefs are influenced by your experiences while growing up, and that they (your beliefs), in turn, influence how you rate your earthly experiences on your spectrum.

Appreciate how easy it is for duality to distort the rules that govern life on Earth, especially rule one. Rule one focuses on equal and opposite actions and reactions. The outcome of combining rule one and duality is you believing and categorizing actions and reactions that you experience as either good or bad. Beyond categorizing your experiences as good or bad, you proceed to assign a degree of magnitude to your perceptions of the experiences, and then place them on some point along your duality spectrum between heaven and hell. This means your experiences can be good, better, best, or heavenly, while others can be bad, worse, worst, or hellish.

The reason you end up categorizing your experiences as good or bad is all thanks to the first unique aspect affecting life on Earth, the feeling of abandonment. Remember, because of abandonment, you experienced an illusionary fear that you are alone resulting from Consciousness abandoning you. The fear left you with no choice but to protect yourself to ensure your survival. In attempting to protect yourself, you had to make sense of your Earth life experience. As you lived, you began to perceive and experience many other feelings and emotions that reminded you of fear, including pain and suffering, to name a few. When this happened, you were left with no choice again but to protect yourself from these feelings, and as you continuously did that, you were unconsciously creating a duality spectrum.

You began to believe that all experiences that reminded you of fear were bad, and you did everything you could to avoid them. On the other hand, the experiences that were void of fear were pleasant to you, and you did everything you could to try to experience them over and over.

It is entirely necessary that you engage in this kind of behavior because it helps keep you safe, amongst other things, so long as you continue to live under the illusion that Consciousness has abandoned you. Even if you do remember that your connection to Consciousness is and has always been there, there is still a need to ensure your survival. The difference is, ensuring your survival as someone who remembers their eternal connection to Consciousness is not riddled with fear.

A little more about your duality spectrum. I know you categorize your earthly experiences on your duality spectrum, based on your perceptions, every single day of your life, so I am not concerned that you will stop any time soon. I also need you to appreciate that, by exercising your right to free will and unconditional love, you unconsciously employ the concept of duality to categorize the actions and reactions you experience as either good or bad. There is nothing wrong with engaging in this type of behavior either. If you recall your earlier readings, however, the actions and reactions are Consciousness' preferred method for maintaining its balance or homeostasis. That is it.

If you understand nothing else from this chapter, please be aware that the act of utilizing your illusionary fears to keep you safe is an essential behavior for you to appreciate as you continue working towards remembering why you are.

So, Why Are the Unique Aspects Important?

It all goes back to Consciousness' ceaseless desire to experience and express infinite emotions, and to exist in an infinite array of forms. The Earth life experience is just another environment that supports a unique type of existence for Consciousness. Although, if I must say so again, it is a brilliantly designed environment to experience life. As far as I am aware, there is no other place in the universe that provides the opportunity to experience fear, duality, and to create a pseudo persona (your ego) like we do here on Earth.

Think about how much ingenuity went into the design of the Earth life experience. Because of these unique aspects, you have the capability to experience life under the illusion that you are separate from everything and everyone. You can experience life as a lonely and abandoned being. You have the capability to experience fear, and you are limitless in what fears you can create and experience. Likewise, you are limitless as to what solutions you can create to overcome the fears. There literally is no end to what you can create and perceive as either fear or its opposite.

As you continue to experience Earth life from a place of fear, everything that you say and do, the beliefs and fears you create, their solutions, and your thoughts provide Consciousness tremendously valuable information about itself. You are helping expand Consciousness through your efforts. You are helping Consciousness remember just how powerful its eternal bond to itself is. You are contributing to the infinite ways Consciousness can exist, express itself, and experience emotions.

I want to take this moment to acknowledge just how brave a soul you are to agree to be part of this experience. In most cases, you have returned to Earth many times to play the game. With each incarnation, particularly this one, you are providing us (all unique expressions of Consciousness) tremendous opportunities to learn and grow towards remembering our limitless selves—our truest nature. You are a vital part of the experience of the entire cosmos, not to mention the experience we know as, Earth life. Seriously, thank you for your contributions, my friend.

By the way, this would be a great point in your reading to retake the Connection to Consciousness assessment you took at the beginning of the book.

Recap of the Unique Aspects Affecting the Illusion of Earth Life

As an environment to experience life, Earth has unique aspects that affect your perceptions of the experience.

All beings experiencing life on Earth must agree to experience the first unique aspect before outgrowing their childhood.

The first unique aspect is the illusion of abandonment. This illusion causes you to believe that Consciousness has abandoned you to fight for and protect yourself. It introduces the illusionary experience/ emotion of fear. It also allows you to experience Earth life as separate from everyone and everything.

The second unique aspect is your ego. Your ego is the character/ avatar that allows you to play the Earth life game. Your ego is your illusionary self that becomes aware of itself after experiencing abandonment. Your ego seeks to make sense of the Earth life experience as it struggles to avoid its illusionary fears.

The third unique aspect is the belief in contraries. Your ego leverages this belief to create your duality spectrum. Extreme ends of your duality spectrum are contraries and may include your subjective believes of God/heaven and Satan/hell. Your duality spectrum is fluid, and changes as your awareness of who you are changes.

5

Earth Life is An Illusion

"The man who has perceived God looks upon all types of men as dream motion-picture images, made of the relativities of the light of Cosmic Consciousness and the shadows of delusion." —Paramahansa Yogananda

My Awakening

I began meditating in my bedroom in Nashville, Tennessee in 2014. You may recall that my first attempt was short, and I fell asleep almost as soon as I began. Still, I kept at the practice. My initial five minutes of meditating soon quickly turned into hours sitting and expanding knowledge of myself. Four years later, on the lovely Tuesday morning of August 21st, 2018, I found myself standing in my kitchen doorway, which leads to my backyard, smiling and laughing in disbelief at the realization that all of Earth life is an illusion. I still had tears in my eyes. I looked outside at the green grass on my lawn, the grey car parked next to my white, aged, storage shed, and the cloud patches scattered underneath the beautiful blue morning sky. I looked at my neighbor's house on my right and her burgundy car parked next to her own storage shed, and then I looked at the photo studio on my left. I felt a gust of wind blow across my face and witnessed its effects on the tall branches and green brushes serving as property boundaries separating my house and the photo studio. I could see and hear cars driving on Main street, about 200 yards away from me. While witnessing all of this, I could barely contain my excitement. I had just remembered that all these things were illusionary unique expressions of me, having a temporary experience, designed to expand Consciousness' knowledge of itself. What a magnificently designed concept. It was unbelievably beautiful. It was the work of pure genius. All I could think, as my eyes darted all over the place, was, *so that's what's going on here.*

Shortly before this moment, I was downstairs in my bedroom meditating. I'd woken up earlier that morning, a little bit after four, as had been routine for me for over four years now. Unlike other mornings when I might have needed to convince myself to meditate, this morning was different. Upon waking up, I had a strong urge to immediately begin meditating. In fact, it was this urge that woke me up.

For about three or four months leading up to this day, there was a specific yoga pose my body would continue to attempt to adopt while I meditated. All my attempts were futile, and I never succeeded in holding the pose for any length of time before falling over. The pose was a tougher version of the boat pose, a sitting and balancing pose requiring core and leg strength, and relaxed muscles. The pose required that I sit on my butt and raise my legs to the sky at a forty-five-degree angle, whilst keeping them straight. I needed to also keep my torso straight, with my head above my shoulders, neck relaxed, and eyes focused ahead of me. To complete the pose, I needed to grab the bottom of my feet with my hands and stabilize myself in this position. In effect, the completed pose looked like an upside-down equilateral triangle balancing on its vertex angle (my butt). The legs of the triangle were my legs and torso, and the base was the connection formed by my hands holding on to the bottom of my feet.

Shortly after I began meditating that morning, my body again attempted to adopt the same yoga pose. This time, and to my surprise, I succeeded in holding the pose long enough for it to have a lasting effect on me. Immediately after balancing myself in the pose, my entire body began to shake and vibrate. At the same time, I felt a rush of energy move up from the base of my spine to the crown of my head. The shaking feeling was unmistakable, and the sensation of the energetic movement up my spine was unlike anything I had ever experienced in my life. I have had one other experience like that since.

With every wave of energetic movement from the base of my spine to my head, I remembered pieces of information about who and why I was. It all happened rapidly. Each time I remembered some aspect of this information, I exclaimed, "A-ha, a-ha. Yes! Yes! Oh, my goodness! So, that's what's going on! I remember!"

I used the word *remember* because that is exactly what the experience felt like. I was not discovering something new that I was never aware of. Instead, I was remembering information that I always knew but, for the very beautiful reasons I discuss in Chapter 4, could not remember. I now laugh in appreciation of why I did not remember: it is part of the Earth life design. The same genius design allowed me to remember by examining all I knew from a different perspective. I realized the perspective whilst meditating that morning.

Put another way, I always knew the information, but it was fragmented, just like pieces in a puzzle set. All the pieces in the set represent pieces of information about who or what the puzzle is. By looking at each piece separately, you might struggle to figure out what the final picture will reveal. Regardless of how you go about it, it is only after putting the pieces together correctly that you are afforded a new perspective to see the puzzle in its entirety. It is from this new perspective that you are able to realize who or what the final image of the puzzle is. This is exactly what happened to me on the lovely morning of Tuesday, August 21st, 2018. I put pieces of the puzzle about the Earth life experience together, which afforded me a new perspective. One of the first things I remembered that morning about why we are was that all of Earth life is an illusionary experience.

Earth Life Really is An Illusion

You know the difference between who you are and who *You* are. You also possess vast knowledge about why you are, including the rules that govern your existence and the unique aspects that distort your perceptions of your existence. If you consider all this information carefully, you should be able to arrive at the conclusion that Earth life is truly an illusion. If you still cannot, allow me to help you start to remember this universal truth.

For starters, you ought to acknowledge the unique and beautiful experience that is life on Earth. Life on Earth is so unique that you cannot experience anything like it anywhere else in the entire universe, as far as I know. I implore you to appreciate that this unique and beautiful experience is marvelous because everything you believe to be complicated about it is, indeed, quite simple. Once you remember this information, because *You* already know it, the whole experience will feel comical. When you remember what is going on, on Earth, you will be left feeling like the punchline to the greatest joke ever. The creativity and genius design (as you have learned in the previous chapter) that goes into making this whole experience possible is second to none. No descriptive words that I am aware of can do it justice. Once you remember this, you will laugh out loud and possibly cry out loud at the same time. I know I did on the Tuesday morning I remembered, and I will never forget the moment.

Life on Earth is not what you have come to believe it to be. Yes, it is unique and beautiful and presents its fair share of challenges in rhythmic fashion that may feel real to you, but the realness is not real at all. Honestly, life on Earth is entirely an illusion. It is real in the same way you might think video games, or your dreams, are real.

I know you have had dreams in your life that felt so real you were either disappointed or elated when you woke up. You may have been disappointed because the dreams were outstanding and you did not want them to end, or you may have been elated because they were nightmares and you were glad when you woke up because waking up meant the end of the dream. After waking up from a nightmare, you likely thought to yourself, *Oh that was just a dream,* and by accepting that it was, you believed the dream was not as real as your Earth life experiences, and therefore worried less about its effects on your earthly being. Well, life on Earth is no different from your dreams.

Life on Earth is truly a dream-like experience. It is truly an illusion. I can best describe this illusion as a school, where all souls, including you, come to learn a wide array of individualized lessons. Life on Earth is also a show or a movie, where all souls, including you, play myriad characters to support their learning. Considering everything I have experienced in my Earth life, all the schooling I have gone through and shows I have seen, I can confidently tell you that life on Earth is the greatest illusionary school, show, or movie ever put together. Oh, I must mention here that life on Earth is the greatest school and show ever put together, in part, because of you. I sincerely thank you for your contributions.

At every moment on Earth, all unique expressions of Consciousness are playing significant roles that contribute to producing this grand illusion. This is not different from how the organs and the myriad parts of your body are all playing essential roles to maintain your body's homeostasis or balance. Your role as an illusionary, individual expression of Consciousness on Earth, regardless of how significant or insignificant you believe it to be, is no more important than any other's. Understanding and accepting how significant or insignificant your role is compared to the roles of other unique expressions of Consciousness merely represents your level of awareness of your connection to Consciousness.

The level of awareness that you possess is unique to you, just as it is for all other unique expressions of Consciousness. If you can imagine combining all these myriad levels of awareness, you can appreciate how they collectively contribute to the current state and perceptions of life on Earth. Our collective awareness takes into account how everyone and everything on Earth experiences and perceives the illusion that is life on Earth. It also explains why we are co-creators of the universe we experience. As co-creators, we employ our thoughts and beliefs to help us think about, act on, and perceive our experiences. As co-creators, our awareness helps us perform actions we find pleasant or worthwhile.

Like I said, the Earth life experience is part of a magnificently designed universal or cosmic illusionary system, which allows Consciousness to feed off itself to better itself. In other words, this cosmic system is pure Consciousness—alive, self-sustaining, and growing exponentially at the same time.

So Why is Life on Earth an Illusion?

Simply put, life on Earth is an illusion because it allows your illusionary self, your ego, to exist and interact with other illusionary expressions of itself. If the Earth life experience were any other way, it could not support who you are. It could not support the fact that you (your ego) are an illusionary, unique expression of *You*, as discussed in Chapter 1.

You can think of it in another way. Why would the real you, *You*, experience life in an imaginary and temporary creation like Earth? There is no need for *You* to do so. *You* experiencing life on Earth, instead of you, would be similar to you *physically* experiencing life in the same universe as Mario from Super Mario Brothers. Because you perceive Mario's world to be an illusion or simulation, I am certain you also understand you cannot physically live in the simulated universe where Mario presides. You can only experience Mario's world by playing a character in that world. Similarly, the character that allows *You* to experience life on Earth is you (your ego).

If you exist, which you do, but unfortunately could not experience life in a universe that supports your frequency of vibration, like the Earth does, you would not be able to support Consciousness' ability to expand knowledge of itself. You would not support why you are. Recall from chapter 2 that one of your purposes for existing is to help yourself expand your consciousness. This, in effect, also helps Consciousness expand its consciousness. Nothing that exists is purposeless and everything that exists needs an environment to support its purpose. This is precisely why Earth is an illusion through and through. It allows the illusionary *You*, your ego, you, to fulfill its purpose.

In the next chapter, I expand on the truth that Earth life is an illusion, by discussing another aspect of the experience that you can only perceive, the way you do, while on Earth.

Recap of Earth Life Is an Illusion

Earth life is an illusionary creation designed to support the existence of you (your ego), an illusionary unique expression of Consciousness.

Earth life is no different from how you currently perceive your dreams, a video game, or a movie. You may continue to believe it to be real, but *You* know it to be an illusion.

Earth life is an illusionary show. All unique expressions of Consciousness experiencing life on Earth are playing important roles that support the show.

Earth life is an illusionary school designed for all souls partaking in the experience to learn uniquely designed lessons. Unlike any other school, all unique expressions of Consciousness experiencing Earth life school are in different grades. The grades represent the unique expression of Consciousness' soul evolution. All the learnings the soul attains on schoolroom Earth provide infinite opportunities for Consciousness to expand knowledge of itself.

6

Time Doesn't Exist

"The distinction between the past, present, and future is only a stubbornly persistent illusion." —Albert Einstein

Now is as good a time as ever to discuss the concept of time (no pun intended), and the role it plays for you as you continue to experience life on Earth. Like duality, time is another exciting aspect and illusion influencing your perceptions of your earthly experiences. Time allows you to separate your life experiences linearly, perceiving them as occurring in the past, the present, and future. It also allows you to perceive that you are experiencing your fears in the same linear fashion, of course. Sadly, time is a leading cause of anxiety for you as it causes you to become anxious when you use it to worry about your ability or inability to attain your ends.

For instance, ceaselessly worrying about any of your future experiences, including meeting work deadlines, having enough money to pay your bills, or the outcome of the football game between your favorite team and another. In the same light, you become anxious when you use your time to reminisce about past pleasant or unpleasant experiences. For example, you could relive your breakup with your first love, the tragic passing of a dear family member, or the time when your co-worker upset you with their comments about your work ethic, or lack of, being detrimental to your employer's goals.

Know that as you continue to relive your past experiences and re-experience their respective emotions, you are permanently living in the past. Couple that with constantly worrying about the future, and you are left with always being absent in the present. In other words, you are not fully vested in what you are or can be doing right now, which severely hinders your ability to express your most authentic emotions in the moment. Appreciate how this is synonymous with acting below you potential. I discuss the importance of always being authentic and acting authentically in Chapter 10.

Your egoic mind is not designed to multitask, as you may have come to believe. You express your infinite creativity best when you focus on your present; when you focus on what is taking place right now. The magnificent soul, teacher, and author Eckhart Tolle does a brilliant job explaining the illusion of time in his book, *The Power of Now.* I strongly recommend that you use some of your "time" to read it.

I also strongly encourage you to understand that you cannot change the past and should, therefore, stop worrying about it. Stop worrying about it in the sense that you may wish to return there to change your actions or something else. Thinking along the same lines, because future events are not happening in the present, you also cannot affect any future events much more than with the actions and decisions you make in the present. This means you need not worry about future events or the theoretical emotions of fear, angst, or anxiety they will evoke within you.

Realize that by being fully present in the present, including being aware of your thoughts and the ones you decide to latch on to, your actions will have a greater chance of reflecting your most authentic feelings and will continue to provide you with glimpses of your most authentic self. That is, with glimpses of living like *You*. This is synonymous to living in bliss. Living in bliss eliminates the need for you to worry about your past or your future. It supports your ability to know and accept that all you can ever affect are your actions after perceiving what *is*, or the present moment.

See, time is not only an illusion, but it is also not quite a unique expression of Consciousness. Time does not exist. No form of Consciousness, Oneness, or Energy exists in the form of time unlike every other thing. What I mean is that you cannot subject time to any of your senses. It is impossible for you to touch, see, hear, taste, or smell time. Try it for yourself and let me know what the outcome of your experiment is. You can neither destroy nor create time, nor can you change it from one form to another. Again, feel free to try this experiment and educate me on the outcome.

Time is no more than an arbitrary measure of Consciousness in motion through space. On Earth, we use time, along with distance and speed, to predict precise locations of where myriad unique expressions of Consciousness will be as they move through space. However, time, like your ego and duality, is unique because it is both a useful and necessary aspect that supports your ability to experience life on Earth. Besides, as far as I am aware, you can only experience time the way you currently do while here on Earth. Time does not exist the way you perceive it to exist outside of Earth. As a matter of fact, if you wrap your head around this universal truth—that time is an arbitrary measure of Consciousness in motion through space—you can also appreciate the idea of everything that is taking place in the entire universe, occurring at the same time. All that is taking place is all happening now.

Nothing happens in the past, and nothing happens in the future. Everything that has ever happened took place in its present, or its now. Similarly, everything that will ever happen will also occur in its present, or its now. The present is all that is and all you need to begin to focus on. As events occur in the present, they occur in perfect synchronicity throughout the entire universe.

I realize this might be a hard concept to grasp, but it is true. Recall that your actions provide opportunities for Consciousness to expand knowledge and awareness of itself. As you engage in your actions in the present, Consciousness instantly learns the information generated from them. Again, I invite you to read Eckhart Tolle's book in your free time. I dedicate only a chapter in this book to the concept of time, while his entire book is dedicated to explaining it.

Time and Physical Changes

You may be wondering why, if time does not exist, you can observe physical changes to your body as you continue to perceive time passing. That is an excellent question to ask yourself, and I invite you to consider the following: consider that time is not the reason why you observe your body changing. Regardless of whether you can perceive time passing, your body will still experience and manifest physical changes.

This is because your body, as a unique expression of Energy, is ceaselessly vibrating at some frequency. Everything around you—your house, couch, family members, dog, electronic devices—are all also vibrating at their unique frequencies. As you continue to expose your body to other frequencies of vibration, an interaction occurs, which results in exchange of information. The exchange of information causes changes to your body's frequency of vibration. These new frequencies of vibration, though minute and insignificant, accumulate over multiple repeated exposures. They end up causing changes to your physical being, and this is what you observe as changes to your body. Your body changes are not dependent on your perception of time.

Higher frequencies of vibration are often the ones you categorize on the pleasant side of your duality spectrum, and lower frequencies are the ones you categorize on the unpleasant side. Exercising and eating healthy foods raise your body's frequency of vibration and change its physical appearance. By healthy foods, I mean foods that have gone through minimal alterations from their natural state up until when you eat them. Additionally, I am referring to foods you would perceive as having low to no emotional intelligence. These foods also contain high levels of unadulterated prana, or life force energy. I discuss the concept of prana further in chapter 14.

Back to the idea of vibrational frequencies: not exercising and eating unhealthy foods lower your body's frequency of vibration and change its physical appearance. Lower frequencies manifest as myriad illness, including headaches, diabetes, and cancer. Again, realize that these physical changes will still manifest as you expose your body to Energies with differing frequencies of vibration, even if you were aware of or lacked the awareness of the perception of time.

Timeless You—*You* (Your Soul)

You believe time exists because your ego identifies with it. Recall that your ego is the part of you living under the illusion that Consciousness has abandoned you. Your ego is also the part of you that identifies with duality and much more. Again, there is absolutely nothing wrong with your ego believing Consciousness abandoned it, identifying with duality or perceiving time, as it is necessary for your ego to believe the lie and employ the illusionary concepts to experience Earth life. They all help keep it safe while you're here on Earth, and as you journey back home to Consciousness.

The real you however—the pure Consciousness that *You* are, have been, and always will be—is your soul. Your soul is the part of you that remembers your eternal connection to Consciousness. Your soul is also the part of you that your ego tries to protect from eternal damnation in hell after your physical body experiences a form of change you know as death. Your ego would rather have your soul end up in Heaven, where it can live for eternity in peace and harmony. The reason you have this belief is because you remember that your soul lives forever and shall never perish. Well, this is true. Now, how long do you think forever, or eternity is? Regardless of your answer, understand that both merely signify the absence of the perception of time. Your soul, which is another unique expression of Consciousness, does not perceive or identify with time.

If your soul, the real you, does not acknowledge the perception of time, why continue to allow the illusionary you, your ego, to be limited by it? It is true that the perception of time is necessary for you to experience life on Earth, and that should be all you use it for. Do not let the perception define your experiences or hinder you from creating the Earth life show you envision for yourself.

Time, the Useful Tool

Be grateful that you can perceive the existence of time as you continue to experience life on Earth. Time truly is a beautiful tool. Many unique expressions of Consciousness understand this and employ it to flex their infinitely creative minds. Consider how astronomers use the concept of time, distance, and speed to predict precise locations of the stars and planets in our solar systems. They leverage this knowledge to predict the occurrences of fascinating phenomena, like solar or lunar eclipses, and they can tell you with high precision where to station yourself on Earth to experience them.

Likewise, engineers, scientists, and astronauts use time to explore the deep parts of space. Astronauts can travel to the moon and build and maintain operations of the International Space Station, thanks in part to their understanding and use of time. Businessmen and women also use time as they work with other unique expressions of Consciousness to express their infinite creativity. Consider how they can work together to construct magnificent buildings with artistic flair unlike any other in the world.

Besides improving travel in space or supporting the construction of inspiringly-designed buildings, you, as a unique expression of Consciousness, can also use time to heal your wounds and overcome your fears. I encourage you to use your time to become intimately familiar with every aspect of who you currently are (what your egoic mind created). Use your time to become aware of your thoughts and unconscious habits or beliefs. Use your time to bring your fears to your conscious awareness so that you can work to overcome them, let them go, or change them. Use your time to learn how your beliefs are limiting you from being the infinitely creative being that you truly are in your purest form. Above all, use your time to remember your eternal connection to Consciousness. I share simple and effective examples of how you can use your time to heal and remember who you truly are in chapter 14.

Anyway, there is no need to rush through remembering who you truly are, because of some fear that you will run out of time. You will never run out of time. Remember, time, like duality, is an arbitrary concept affecting your perceptions of your earthly experiences. Also, just as Consciousness does not identify with duality, know that it also does not identify with time. Become present in every moment of your life and recognize how time becomes less of a factor for you. In other words, relax in your current skin. You literally have eternity to remember why you are.

Perceiving No Time on Earth

I am sure you have experienced moments in your life when you perceived time to be absent, or when time was not a factor in your immediate present/experience. Those experiences exemplify your living in bliss or being fully present in the present. They represent moments when your focus was entirely on what you were doing.

An example of this would be closing your eyes to take a quick nap, only to wake up many hours later. I am sure you woke up feeling perplexed about what had just happened. You might have wondered how you could've closed your eyes for a second, only to have all that time pass, or wondered how it was possible for your blink to equate to three hours of your Earth life. If the above example does not resonate with you, consider the following.

There have been many episodes in my life when I showed up to work early in the morning and immediately became involved in the tasks I needed to complete. After what felt like a short while at work, I glanced at the clock in my office and realized it was already time for lunch. Four to five hours had passed, and I could not come to grips with where the time had gone.

Similar perceptions of no time on Earth are particularly true for parents. A parent fully vested in being present for their child(ren)'s growth recognizes the phenomenon of the absence of time. Shortly after their child is born, they may worry that there is not enough time to spend with them before they must return to work or before the child starts their first days of school. The reality of the absence of time hits home with more gravitas as they witness their child(ren) reaching milestones—graduating, getting married, and especially becoming parents themselves.

If none of the above examples resonate with you, try the following: find the oldest picture of you. One that captured you closest to the day you were born. A baby picture is the best option. Review your life from the day you believe the picture was taken up until today— the day you are reading this sentence. I am sure you can appreciate that the time flew by quickly. In other words, "Where did the time go?"

The truth is, time went nowhere, because it really was never there; however, if you must insist on the existence of time, then it has always been present, but only in the now. All that changed for you was how you perceived its presence or lack of.

It is essential to understand this point because your perceptions of time inform your attitude toward and ability to be present, and to express your most authentic feelings in the moment, or in the now. You are aware of the expression, "time flies when you are having fun." The expression is correct to a certain degree. If you continue to be adamant about the existence of time, then you must agree that measuring it does not change it. The measure of a second passing is always equal to the standard measure of a second. The idea of time flying means only that you have an altered perception of the second passing.

I would like you to know that as a unique expression of Consciousness experiencing Earth life, you have full authority to choose how you wish to use and perceive time. Also, regardless of how you decide to use it, know that, to Consciousness, you can never be wrong. Whatever you do with your time will continue to provide Consciousness valuable learnings about its infinitely creative self. It is precisely why you are here.

Recap of Time

Time does not really exist. It is an arbitrary tool you use to measure Consciousness in motion.

Time is, however, a necessary tool available to you as you experience life on Earth. It supports your ability to create and experience emotions, which expands your consciousness.

Nothing happens outside of the present moment. The future, the present, and the past all occur in their now.

Focus on being present in your present to improve your perception of your Earth life experiences (to begin to experience life in bliss). This allows you to express you most creative imaginations.

Use more of your time to expand knowledge of yourself, less of it worrying about the future, and even less of it worrying about the past.

Do not let the perception of time define your earthly experiences.

7

You Can Do No Wrong

"Out beyond ideas of wrong-doing and right-doing, there
is a field. I'll meet you there." —Rumi

I f you are reading the title of this chapter and are currently a
parent, you must be thinking I have lost my mind, I have no
clue what I am talking about, and no one in their right minds
should have allowed me to publish this book. If you are not a parent,
you are probably thinking, *Where the heck was this information when
my parents were scolding me for doing something wrong?* Heck, they
may still be scolding you today, as an adult, about your perpetual
and uncanny ability to keep doing wrong. Who am I kidding? I am
sure your entire universe reminds you every day. If not your family,
your friends do. If not your friends, you coworkers or customers,
and even strangers, do.

After all you have read so far, however—including the universal
truth that Consciousness loves you unconditionally—this new universal
truth should not be much of a shock for you to begin to understand.

You may even be wishing that maybe, just maybe, there is a possibility I am referring to a different type of wrongdoing in the title. I can assure you that is not the case.

From the perspective of Consciousness, Oneness, Energy, it is unfeasible for you, or any other unique expression of itself, to do anything wrong. If you forgot already, I would like to take this opportunity to remind you of rule number two governing everything and everyone that is experiencing life on Earth: Consciousness bestows upon all unique expressions of itself unconditional love and free will to do as they please.

I do sympathize with you on how challenging it is to wrap your mind around this truth, and beyond continuing to remind you and provide examples to prove it, there is nothing else I can do. You alone will need to find a solution that eventually supports your understanding and belief of this truth. Consciousness truly does love you unconditionally, and it will continue to love you unconditionally, forever, without care of what you do.

See, unconditional love means love with no conditions. It means love that is not limited by time, by your location, by your thoughts, your actions, or anything your egoic mind can come up with. Unconditional love means you need not do anything for Consciousness to love you. You can do everything and anything, and Consciousness will still love you unconditionally. Solely because you are, because you exist, Consciousness loves you unconditionally.

If these explanations still do not close the chasms that exist between the new you that is starting to believe this statement and the current or old you that vehemently doubts it, consider the second part of rule number two, the declaration of your right to free will. Without this additional statement to remind you of the limitless love Consciousness has for you, maybe you could come up with an argument against its validity. Nonetheless, consider how foolish and confusing it would be if Consciousness declared that it loved you unconditionally, but you were not free to do as you pleased as you continued to experience life on Earth.

First, can you appreciate how not being free to do as you pleased would severely limit your Earth life experiences? I am sure you would agree with me that, if your actions were limited in any way at all, the idea of unconditional love would be negated. By limiting your actions, no one or nothing can declare that they love you unconditionally. Limiting your actions is equivalent to conditional love.

Neither you nor Consciousness, if you continue to believe you are separate from it, can have it both ways. Consciousness cannot love you unconditionally if you do only certain things, in certain ways. The inclusion of the word *if* in any such declaration introduces conditions. But my friend, there are absolutely zero conditions you need to satisfy to receive Consciousness' unconditional love.

Right now, you can either believe that Consciousness loves you unconditionally and grants you free will to do as you please, or you can choose to continue to believe the lie that you are unworthy of this kind of love. You can continue to believe you are somehow so special from all other unique expressions of Consciousness that you are the exception to the rule. Remember, however, that rules one and two have no exceptions. That said, the ball is entirely in your court. Ironically, your access to unconditional love and free will means you can decide that you do not have access to either. I was not kidding when I said the Earth life experience is a comical one!

I can think of two reasons that would explain why you struggle to accept the universal truth that you are, as you are, always worthy of unconditional love. You should be able to guess the first one by now, which is that you continue to live under the illusion that you are separate from Consciousness. The second reason is an outcome of the first one: you continue to identify with your ego to help you make sense of your Earth life experiences.

Your ego, with its limited understandings of who you truly are, believes you are not only separate and alone, but also that you are inferior to a creator. Recall that your ego also identifies with the concept of duality. As a quick reminder, duality is that unique aspect of Earth life that lets you classify actions and reactions as either pleasant or unpleasant.

Your ego employs duality to help you avoid any unpleasant experiences, or any experiences that remind it of fear, as it continues to protect itself. Furthermore, your ego is so creative that it finds ways to combine its beliefs of being inferior to its creator with influences from duality to create new beliefs. The new beliefs are the ones that cause you to believe that, by partaking in pleasant actions only, you are ensuring the creator you believe in views you in a positive light. Alternatively, by partaking in unpleasant actions, the creator's nemesis you believe in (and fear) will now be the one viewing you in a positive light.

You must understand that your ideas of right and wrong, or your duality spectrum, are not only unique to you, but they are also outcomes of your beautiful mind's creativity. They are the outcome of your ability to justify your actions. Justifying your actions is a beautiful and creative way for you to express yourself, which supports Consciousness' learning of itself. Further, justifying your actions are definite proof of the subjectivity that defines what you and all other unique expressions of Consciousness perceive to be pleasant or unpleasant Earth life experiences.

Justifying your actions is perfectly normal, and a necessity for anyone experiencing Earth life under the illusion that Consciousness has abandoned them. Even if you do not realize or accept it as true, I am confident that you would agree you engage in this sort of behavior daily. You justify your actions so much, it is now second nature to you. You have turned it into an art, and you are Picasso's inspiration in this field. Bravo, my friend.

Your uncanny ability to justify your actions before engaging in them, even the actions you believe would result in Satan gaining control of all or a part of your soul, is so out-of-this world ingenious, it is downright comical. Truthfully speaking, it is comical. What you need to realize is this: your ideas of right or wrong beliefs, thoughts, actions, or behaviors are starkly different from how Consciousness perceives all of them. Allow me to explain.

Means to an End

Consciousness maintains a perception of bliss toward everything that every unique expression of itself throughout the entire cosmos, including planet Earth, thinks, says, or does. This blissful perception never waivers. It is as constant as the idea that creation and change (transformation) are inevitable. It is as reliable as the knowledge that tomorrow is now much closer to being here than ever before. It is the only way to best explain what the idea of unconditional love really means. It is the best and most reliable way to explain and understand why you are free to do as you please at any time you are consciously aware of your existence. And it is true.

Consciousness does not identify with egoic constructs of pleasant vs. unpleasant experiences, good vs. bad feelings or emotions, or right vs. wrong. To Consciousness, there is no such thing. Consciousness views every single action—including thoughts, words, or deeds that every single unique expression of itself throughout the entire cosmos engages in—as no more than a neutral means to an end for that unique expression of itself. This is a universal truth. A means to an end is all Consciousness perceives and cares about. This is another excellent place to stop and take a breather, if you need to, before proceeding.

Just so we are on the same page about what a "means to an end" means, understand that a means represents everything you experience while on your path to achieving your end. Your means is your path, and it includes your thoughts, your words, your actions, your beliefs, and everything you can imagine that was part of your experience towards achieving your end. Your end, on the other hand, is your goal, or your heaven. I will provide a very simple example to illustrate what I mean by the path you engage in to meet your end.

Your end in the following example is your wish/desire to have ice cubes available at your home for your guests who are coming over to watch the Super Bowl. Your path or means include the infinite thoughts, words and actions you can have, say, and engage in to ensure that you have ice cubes at your house by the time your guests arrive for the Super Bowl.

Now, because you continue to live in fear and believe that your creator prefers you to engage in only pleasant behaviors, you limit the words and actions you can engage in to have ice at your house for your guests. This belief of your creator's preferences might even cause you to feel guilty by becoming aware of an unpleasant thought on the methods you should engage in to obtain the ice. For instance, you might question your sanity if while working hard to obtain the ice, your thoughts included the idea of robbing the convenience store in your neighborhood at gunpoint and walking away with two free bags of ice.

If the outcome of the thought alone was you feeling guilty, we can both agree that actually engaging in the action is out of the question. Nothing and no one can convince you to rob a convenience store at gun point for two free bags of ice cubes for your Super Bowl party because your egoic mind's past experiences and current beliefs are causing you to believe this method or action would not be worth the reactions you would experience. Is going to jail worth two bags of ice? Absolutely not. It is an unpleasant experience. You would much rather walk into the convenience store, pick up two bags of ice, make your way to the cashier's register and pay for them. You would probably share a few pleasantries with the cashier before going home to be with your guests as host of the Super Bowl party.

I want to reassure you of this universal truth, however. Consciousness could care less how you ensured there was ice at your house for your guests, so long as you were authentic while engaging in them (even if you weren't). You could have decided to rob the convenience store at gun point, killed the cashier, walked out to your vehicle with two free bags of ice in your hands, and driven home, and Consciousness would have still loved you unconditionally. Alternatively, you could have paid for the ice and made your way home, like you did, and still, Consciousness would continue to love you unconditionally.

Neither actions would have damned your soul to hell or saved a space for it in heaven or purgatory or anywhere else. No such place exists but in the vast, infinite, constructs of your creative mind. What results from either of your actions is what rule number one declares. Consciousness will experience an equal and opposite reaction to ensure that it stays in a hemostatic state—the Consciousness balance. Additionally, Consciousness' knowledge of itself will expand, which is precisely why you are (to help it expand... – I am confident you understand this by now).

You know this to be true already; you just do not remember. You have experienced many moments in your life when you are so focused on attaining your end that you moved on your path with an attitude of neglect towards what you have come to believe as moral rights or wrongs. In those moments, you were acting from a space and perspective that is similar to how Consciousness always perceives itself. This perception is what I keep referring to as bliss.

Additionally, those moments provided a glimpse of how you can perceive your entire Earth life experiences once you remember who you truly are, which is pure Consciousness. When your path is void of your manufactured moral rights and wrong, you have engaged in one of two things. You have either found a creative way to justify your actions as right, or you have found a creative way to convince yourself that you are ready and willing to deal with the reactions that are the outcome of your actions. In other words, you've convinced yourself that the future reactions you experience are worth the current actions that you are about to engage in, though you may perceive them as unpleasant, or as reminiscent of your fears.

Another reason why right and wrong are entirely constructs of your own mind's creativity is the differing opinions and advice you receive from your friends, families, or colleagues. Think back to a time when you have been unsure about engaging in an action or behavior that you knew your perceptions would render unpleasant. If you are like most folks, you likely sought advice from your social circle about what to do.

Now, think back to the advice you sought from your closest friends and family about your dilemma. I am confident you would agree the advice you received was as varied as the number of people you sought advice from. The reason for this is they all provided you what *they* thought you should do, as filtered through their personal conditionings. By *conditionings*, I mean their personal earthly experiences that have helped shape their beliefs and perceptions of right and wrong. If you can, please appreciate that all the advice you received was also influenced by their fears and came from a space of needing to protect themselves primarily. In situations where your duality spectrum differed from the person providing you advice, it likely rendered their advice for you as an outright contradiction to what you believed to be your preferred mode of action.

Truthfully, it is a marvelous experience to observe the contradictions that individuals who continue to live in fear exhibit daily. It really is a work of art and is essentially why the Earth life experience is the greatest show ever put together.

One example that demonstrates the contradictions that are the outcome of continuing to live in fear is if you consider yourself to be a Christian who firmly ascribes to the teachings of the Christian faith but decide to enlist in the army during a time of war. In such times, you are aware of the increased likelihood that you may have to deploy into a war zone to fight your enemies. At the same time, you are also aware of your Christian teachings that strongly condemn the act of killing, and instead, promote the need to learn to be accepting and tolerant of everyone, despite your perceived differences.

Firmly aware of both, you nonetheless proceed to enroll in the army and are comfortable with your imminent deployment. You and numerous likeminded unique expressions of Consciousness now find yourselves in a war zone with fully loaded assault rifles and other weapons—shooting, bombing, and doing anything you can imagine to defeat your enemy and ensure your survival (your means to your end). To be fair, your enemy is also doing everything they can to kill you, *their* enemy, and ensure their survival (their means to their end).

Now, how did you end up in a war zone, armed and ready to kill a fellow unique expression of Consciousness, while simultaneously believing that killing is an unpleasant experience, and one that would bring you closer to your creator's nemesis and further away from your creator? The answer is simple. You succeeded in leveraging your mind's infinite creativity to believe your actions were justifiable for some reason, whatever the reason may be.

By the way, I am not your moral guru. I must declare that whatever you choose to do while experiencing life on Earth is entirely your choice. From the perspective of Consciousness, you can do no wrong.

Killing is an extreme action to engage in and an excellent type of behavior to use to drive home the point that you can do no wrong. That is why I keep employing it in my examples. Though I use killing as a teaching tool, I want you to be aware that I, personally, do not condone the behavior.

Back to making my point. I am sure you can agree that the myriad heartbreaking and emotional atrocities that are very much part of the history of humanity on Earth provide a great deal of learning and teaching to Consciousness. The outcome of these violent experiences in our past has been the expansion of Consciousness. The violence has caused many unique expressions of Consciousness to remember who they truly are, and their eternal connection to everything and everyone.

Because Consciousness experienced the violence, pain, and suffering it inflicted upon itself, appreciate that, over time, Consciousness learned to express more love, compassion, and care to itself throughout the cosmos. This is not only true, it is also an important universal truth for you to become aware of.

As far as not being able to ever do anything wrong, I am sure you would agree with the fact that Adolf Hitler and his actions provided a vast amount of teaching and learning opportunities for Consciousness. Consider that during Adolf Hitler's reign as chancellor of Germany, the Germans rose to power and became a prosperous and powerful country, not only throughout Europe, but also throughout the world. I am sure they collectively basked in their supremacy, though there might have been a good number of Germans who were not too pleased with Hitler's modus operandi. If you can, please appreciate how everything the Germans did under Hitler's reign to attain their dominance represented a means to an end for them. Engaging in multiple wars was a means to an end for the German government.

The despicable acts, atrocities, and treatments that Jews in Germany experienced under Hitler's reign constituted means for the German government to attain its end. No matter how disgusting you perceive the acts to be, I hope you can find it in yourself to appreciate that an equal amount of the opposite resulted from them. Rule number one is proof that an equal amount and magnitude of what the Jews endured under Hitler's reign resulted from the actions. If you are not convinced, consider that because these experiences occurred, not only is Consciousness much closer to itself than ever before, but there has also been no other unique expression of itself attempt to gain dominance over others by employing the same methods Hitler did.

No collective unique expressions of Consciousness are experiencing conditions as vile as the concentration camps the Jews in Germany had to endure. Since Consciousness' awareness of itself and infinite creativity continues to be apparent, appreciate how the techniques used to gain dominance these days, just like the weapons used to fight in today's wars, are more complex and efficient, respectively, than they have ever been before. This is also precisely a desire of Consciousness—to exist in ever-more complex forms.

The actions of the German government under Hitler's rule were not the only atrocities to provide a vast amount of teaching and learning opportunities to Consciousness. Other historical atrocities, including the slave trade and the Bible story of Master Jesus, also provided tremendous opportunities for Consciousness.

Master Jesus

As far back as I can remember, the stories about Master Jesus have fascinated me. I think it is amazing that, after over 2000 years, many brave souls experiencing Earth life today continue to revere him as the only son of God. These brave souls who continue to live in fear because they do not remember who they truly are, perceive Master Jesus as separate and superior to them. They perceive Master Jesus as always perfect and the only person capable of talking to their creator on their behalf. They believe it is only through Master Jesus that they can secure a place in heaven for their inferior souls and avoid eternity in hell.

Now, there is absolutely nothing wrong with holding onto these beliefs. I held onto similar beliefs and understandings of who I was until I began to question them. I briefly mentioned in the preface how my skepticism towards religion, amongst other things, played the role of a catalyst for me to begin meditating. After I remembered who I truly was on the lovely Tuesday morning of August 21st, 2018, my understandings of the universal truths changed all the beliefs I held about Master Jesus. Today, I can tell you that Master Jesus was not very different from you. Master Jesus was a unique expression of

Consciousness, like you. He differed because he remembered who he truly was, which is pure Consciousness, and learned to work with myriad vibrations of Energy.

Many renowned researchers and scholars have written excellent books supporting or casting doubt on Master Jesus' life stories. The topics range from whether or not the stories were true or fabricated, to whether they were altered, either intentionally or unintentionally, from the original scripts. I encourage you to read any of them with the same open mind you are keeping as you read this book. My intention for discussing Master Jesus here is to focus on the Bible stories about him. I hope to provide you with enough information to consider how perfect Master Jesus really was, if he was genuinely born without original sin, and if he succeeded in living his entire life without ever sinning.

I discuss Master Jesus here so you can reflect on the belief that he is the only son of God who died on the cross to save you because you are inferior to him and cannot save yourself. Just so we are on the same page, I consider a sin to be an immoral action, as perceived by a (any) unique expression of Consciousness. In other words, a sin is an act—be it a thought, word uttered, or action taken—that you would likely categorize as unpleasant on your duality spectrum. And yes, I do recognize that categorizing experiences as either pleasant or unpleasant is entirely subjective.

To begin, consider that Master Jesus was a human like you. Another human, Mary, gave birth to him here on Earth, in a manger. Second, consider that he actually was here on Earth, where the same two universal rules that govern all earthly experiences would have applied to him like they apply to you. Further, while experiencing life on Earth, Master Jesus was also subject to the three unique aspects that contribute to distorting our perceptions of our experiences —abandonment, the creation of the ego, and duality. Considering the above three points, it should be easy to conclude the Master Jesus was no different from you. It should be impossible to conclude that for thirty-three years, Master Jesus, through all his actions and experiences, was able to avoid being the source of sin. It should be impossible to conclude that, for his entire life, you and your infinitely creative mind are not able to perceive any of his actions as immoral or riddled with unpleasantness.

If you continue to believe his actions were never the source of sin, please enlighten me by sharing what types of actions Master Jesus engaged in that were always immaculate. Before you do, consider this truth. For anyone who continues to live in fear, no action on Earth is solely good and none is solely evil. This means that without a doubt, Master Jesus's actions and experiences while on Earth were simultaneously and equally as perfect as they were imperfect. This is true, and it is no different for you, as you, too, engage in experiences and take myriad actions while here on Earth.

With your infinitely creative mind and right to free will, you can choose to perceive the many amazing and inspiring miracles Master Jesus performed as either good or evil. If you continue to identify with duality, that statement should resonate as true for you. Know that as long as Master Jesus performed the miracles on Earth, I assure you there was an equal amount of opposite reactions that resulted from them, thanks to rule one. Rule number one declares that Consciousness always maintains its balance. Again, this should resonate as true for you, especially if you continue to live in fear. Also, if you continue to live in fear, then you can appreciate how easily you can perceive the opposite reactions that ensured Consciousness' balance as unpleasant or wrong.

If you understand all this, I invite you to leverage both your identification with duality and your infinitely creative mind to come up with stories that illustrate how Master Jesus' miracles could be perceived as unpleasant or wrong. In order words, come up with stories that make you perceive Master Jesus' actions as those you would categorize on the unpleasant side of your duality spectrum. I will share one to illustrate.

I am sure you are familiar with the Bible story recounting Jesus' first miracle where he succeeded in changing water to wine at a wedding. Consider that one of the wedding guests, a lovely and reserved woman in her late thirties, was married to a man who could not control his alcohol consumption. The man was in his mid-forties and was known within the community as a drunk—one who would become belligerent and violent after drinking, often to the distress of his timid wife. Not only was his violence towards his wife cause enough for concern, he also mirrored the exact same behavior towards his kids. Amongst the many reasons he behaved in this manner, one was that he suffered from liver cirrhosis, and could not cope with the fact that the illness was severe. Liver cirrhosis and alcohol are a combination from hell. Alcohol worsens and speeds up the progression of the disease.

Now, imagine you were the lovely lady at the wedding, comforted by the knowledge there was no more alcohol to serve the guests. Put in the same position, you would be calm knowing there was nothing to speed up the inevitable trauma of facing violent attacks from your husband, or of fighting to protect your kids from your violent husband. Now, how calm would you feel after learning that, thanks to Master Jesus, there is a fresh barrel of the finest wine in the country at the wedding? See, this is just one of a literally infinite number of stories you can create to illustrate how any of the guests at the wedding could perceive Master Jesus' actions as unpleasant.

Never forget what you are about to read next. Master Jesus was a brave soul and a unique expression of Consciousness, exactly like you truly are. Master Jesus remembered this universal truth about who we all are, and that is where you, who continue to live in fear, differ from him. You may continue to believe that Master Jesus never sinned, and that's fine, but I hope my example above proved otherwise. I do love examples, though, and can share another one that proves that Master Jesus' life was also a source of unpleasantness.

According to the stories in the Bible, Master Jesus' actions were so despicable that members of his community could not stand the sight of him. Master Jesus' actions infuriated them so much they arrested him, tried him, and found him not guilty. Now most people would let things go at that point—you know, water under the bridge. But no. With Master Jesus, the frustrations were so deep that the people ignored the law of the land and their King's rulings and killed him anyway.

Reflect on the previous sentence for a while, please. Master Jesus made people so mad that they ignored the laws of the land in their time to ensure that he did not live to see another day. Mind you, he was only thirty-three years old when he died. Only thirty-three! Even two thousand years ago, life expectancy was more than thirty-three years, so we cannot use that as an explanation for his death.

Back to the part of the story where the people ignored the King's ruling. Consider how fascinating this is. If the king understood that Jesus was a godly being who was not guilty of any wrongdoing, why did he not fight harder to stop the mob from murdering a truly innocent person? What sort of king was he to set this sort of precedent for the rest of his reign?

Besides knowing that the mob killed Master Jesus innocently, knowing that they killed him the same way they killed two other law-breaking citizens of the time should infuriate you. Today, the ultra-wealthy members of our societies who are guilty of going against society's laws usually spend time under arrest in the most expensive residencies and properties, instead of county or federal prisons. Their punishments are different.

Anyway, getting back to the perspective of the king, consider that it is entirely possible the king did not fight harder to save Master Jesus because, maybe, Master Jesus was not so perfect, immaculate, pure, and void of sin after all. Maybe. And at this point, if you are screaming in your mind that the mob did not know what they were doing by their actions, because even Jesus declared so when he asked the creator to forgive them, stop immediately. All that represents is your infinite ability to justify, and that is it. The mob were fully aware and conscious of their actions.

A New Perspective on the Story of Master Jesus

I do appreciate that the Bible stories of Master Jesus are a source of tremendous inspiration to many souls currently experiencing Earth life. Heck, at some point in my life, they were of great inspiration to me. They provided me guidance, taught me ethics, and helped keep me safe. To truly understand who and why you are, however, you need to begin understanding the story from a new perspective. Try it by closing your eyes and visualizing what the stories recount.

They claim Master Jesus, a unique expression of Consciousness, was alive during some period of our past. You might say he was not just a unique expression of Consciousness, he was the son of God. Okay. If so, the son of God was alive during some period of our past here on Earth. As he lived on Earth, he took it upon himself to remind members of his communities, (mere mortals who drew the short end of the stick and ended up less than sons of God) who they truly were, through his teachings. Master Jesus' teachings included stories, riddles, and metaphors that were pertinent to the times. I, today, can appreciate that, since he lived in bliss, he never became frustrated at the fact that members of his communities did not fully grasp his teachings. All that caused him to do was continue to leverage his infinitely creative mind to create even more valuable teachings, stories, and metaphors. Put another way, it gave him purpose and a sense of job security.

Even with his improved ability to explain these same universal truths to members of his community that I am now also sharing with you, many still did not understand. The Bible stories explain that, instead of working harder to understand, they identified with the feelings they experienced that reminded them of fear, or of Consciousness abandoning them. This means they had no other choice but to create a heaven for themselves.

That heaven, as you already know, was making sure Jesus did not live to experience his thirty-fourth year on Earth. Appreciate how they were able to convince themselves that if Jesus was no longer living amongst them and preaching to them, they would somehow not experience any fear-based feelings or emotions. Not only is that depressing, absurd, and a sad reality of the egoic mind, it also proves just how infinitely creative you are. That is not the end of the story, however, as it gets even better.

Mind you that all of this occurred on Earth, where duality affects everyone's perception of every experience. It occurred in a place where so long as you continue to live under the illusion Consciousness abandoned you, no attempt to attain your heaven will cause you to feel permanently safe. No attempt, my friend. Here is another universal truth. The feeling of being safe is only temporary.

For the members of Jesus' community that killed Master Jesus, a dead Master Jesus only resulted in a safe feeling for a brief period of time; it was definitely temporary, as it soon created a hell for them to contend with. The hell was feelings of shame, guilt, fear, embarrassment, and a plethora of other unpleasant emotions you can think of. If you are following along closely, you now know the next logical thing for these members to do was to find another creative solution to experience heaven again. I must admit, the new solution they created was a beauty. So beautiful that, after two thousand years, many souls experiencing Earth life today continue to ascribe to the same solution. You know the solution all too well.

To really appreciate why it is necessary to view this story from a new perspective, imagine if you experienced all of it in the present time. Imagine that Master Jesus is alive and well today, and you can listen to him provide his teachings in person. Per the story, because you are part of the group of folks that listen to him and cannot understand his teachings, you believe them to be wrong, blasphemous, and riddled with all sorts of fears your creative mind can construct. You identify with the fears and feed them so ceaselessly that they consume your entire life with frustration.

You become livid and cannot stand the sight, voice, or even thought of Master Jesus continuing to scare you with his teachings. So, you and the other folks having similar types of perceptions of unpleasant experiences because of Master Jesus' teachings decide to kill him by, let's say, electrocuting him (modern method of killing).

You work with a member of his inner circle to devise a fail-proof plan that will put Master Jesus in a vulnerable place where you can readily arrest him. After arresting him, you take him through trials, where the courts acquit him of all the charges you levied against him. At this, you realize he could be free to continue spreading his blasphemous stories, so you do everything in your power to ensure authorities do not release him. Nothing and no one can convince you that Master Jesus is innocent. You wholeheartedly believe you can only feel safe if Master Jesus experiences death by electrocution.

You relentlessly (your means) pursue your wish that Jesus ends up dead (your end). And one day, you experience your wish. You are one of an exclusive number of folks seated in a row of benches across from a see-through glass that separates you from a room. In the room is an electrocution chair, and on it, is a strapped-up Master Jesus. From the bench, you and the other folks have a front-row view of an exhausted but blissful Master Jesus as he takes his last breaths after receiving a lethal dose of electricity.

Before he dies, Master Jesus' last words are him declaring his innocence and standing firm that his beliefs and teachings are universally true. He also expresses remorse as to how you are letting fear blind you from this reality and forgives you for you have no idea what you are doing. You ignore him as he speaks. He dies a short moment later.

You and everyone watching attain your heaven. However, because you are on Earth, the heaven you experience is only temporary and succeeds in still creating a fear for you to contend with. You wonder if there is a possibility that he is not entirely dead. So, like the Bible's Master Jesus was stabbed with a spear, you demand that he receive, in addition to the lethal dose of electricity, a lethal injection cocktail. The previously dead Master Jesus is now deader than before. Perfect. Now you are safe from all the frightening thoughts, words, actions, and teachings of Master Jesus. Come one now, let us be real. You are on Earth, so you know you really are not safe, right? That safe feeling you felt after witnessing Jesus die, and then die again, was only a temporary illusion.

Doubt begins to engulf your mind and only continues to grow as time passes beyond the day Master Jesus died twice. You wonder if you have made the biggest mistake in your life. You wonder why you cannot find peace and bliss even after Master Jesus is no longer alive spreading his bullshit beliefs about who and why you truly are. You wonder if you really killed someone special. Your creative mind needs to make sense of it but cannot.

Coupled with the fact that you were already living in fear and believe yourself to be inferior to your creator, you can appreciate how these feelings of guilt, fear, and doubt have no chance whatsoever of providing you access to a permanent state of feeling safe. Except, at last, your creative mind finds an explanation that you think will succeed in keeping you safe. You know the explanation and justification all too well. Like I said, this new belief is a beauty.

You decide and firmly believe that you truly are inferior to the creator. This same creator is the one who created you in his image and loves you unconditionally. The creator also knows that you are inferior to it (the creator), so it sends someone special to save you from yourself. That someone special was Master Jesus after all. The same Master Jesus that you could not stand the sight of and did all you could to kill (twice). However, you now believe killing him was part of the plan, and you were simply playing your role, just like Master Jesus was playing his role. Unlike Master Jesus however, you did not know you were going to kill him as part of the plan, but Master Jesus knew he was going to die by your hands as part of the plan.

And in all the confusion, you conclude that the Master Jesus you killed was the only son of God, and that he was the only one capable of saving you. You conclude that accepting Master Jesus as your savior was the one condition you needed to become worthy of the creator's unconditional love. You believe that Master Jesus, who you killed, was dying to save you. Let that sink in for a moment, please. You believe that Master Jesus, who you killed, willingly died to save you. This is odd, is it not? Did he willingly die or were there moments when he attempted to defend his innocence throughout his trials, you know, moments that you ignored?

Realize that by revering Master Jesus as your one and only true savior, you have given up on actually understanding his teachings. Think how creative you are, that you can convince yourself the person you killed is now the only one capable of saving you. Think how creative you are that you can firmly believe that Master Jesus is the only one able to guarantee you end up in Heaven, because by killing him, he was— wait for it—dying for you. You believe that, in death, Master Jesus was saving you and the people who incarnated on Earth before him. For every soul that incarnates after you killed him, however, you believe they must accept him as their savior, or they will end up in hell for eternity.

However, wait. You are on Earth dealing with duality, and so even believing this new creative solution does not bring you any closer to living in bliss or remembering the truth of who and why you are. So, you create another solution to protect yourself. You are not content with just saving your own soul by accepting Master Jesus as your savior.

No! You become a crusader for him and his teachings. You employ your infinitely creative mind to spread your beliefs about who and what Master Jesus is across the globe, under the guise that you want to save others (know that you are really trying to save yourself). You continue to spread your incorrect understandings to the world, using methods that even you would categorize on the unpleasant/negative side of your duality spectrum.

The outcomes of your efforts are colossal conflicts and tragic violence between you and others with conflicting beliefs. Many innocent souls die, including the souls who remember who and why they truly are. To you, their death is justified because they refused to accept your creator as the one and only creator, whose abode is reserved for those who accept his only son, Master Jesus, as their savior.

Consider this simple question. By engaging in violence that results in your killing innocent people who do not convert to your teachings, do you genuinely believe that you are saving them from their fears? Alternatively, do you genuinely believe that you are saving yourself from your fears?

Your Justifications are Creative Expressions

This reflection on Master Jesus should remind you of your infinite ability to use your creativity to justify your actions. Use your creativity to explain who was right or wrong in the story of Master Jesus. Was the mob right for killing him? Was the mob wrong for killing him? Remember that you cannot be wrong in your answer. Also realize that neither the mob nor Master Jesus was solely either. They were both playing their roles, as illusionary and non-illusionary unique expressions of Consciousness, and they played their roles perfectly.

Consciousness' perspective on the whole scenario is simple. Everything that happened— the actions of the mob and the actions of

Master Jesus—was nothing more than a neutral means to an end for themselves. By engaging in the actions, both the mob and Master Jesus were expanding their consciousness, teaching all of Consciousness how to be infinitely creative, and helping all of Consciousness remember who they truly are. That is it. No one was right, and no one was wrong.

Recognize that the stories of Master Jesus are a great teacher, and the teachings are confusing to anyone who continues to live under the illusion that Consciousness abandoned them. This is true. If you do not believe me, research how many Christian religions exist that use the Bible as their source of all information related to salvation and, unfortunately, have conflicting beliefs with one another. The conflicting beliefs arise merely because they reflect the religion's teachers' current level of awareness of their connection to Consciousness—of who and why they truly are.

Remember, all unique expressions of Consciousness, regardless of their faith, creed, or religion, hold varying levels of this awareness. I cannot stress enough the importance of recognizing that there is absolutely nothing wrong with this diversity of awareness, as it contributes to the collective perceptions of experiences of life on Earth and the entire cosmos.

Still, begin to come to grips with the understanding that Master Jesus is not the savior you think he is. You may employ his teachings as you understand them to help you remember your eternal connection to Consciousness, but only you can save yourself, if at all you think you need saving. It is no different from understanding the value your favorite schoolteachers provided you. They gave you the tools you needed to be a better student. Only you could take the final test, not the teachers. Only you could pass the exams, graduate and integrate your knowledge in the world, not the teachers.

Outcome of Justifying

Know that as you continually live in fear on Earth, you perpetually justify your actions, even when you hold beliefs that would categorize the actions on the negative side of your duality spectrum, which should cause you to avoid them. You perpetually advise yourself with lies so you can take actions you believe will either protect you or provide you satisfaction in the moment. You need not look any further than how competing news media outlets cover the same stories, especially if they are politically related, to observe this phenomenon. You need not look any further than the story of Master Jesus, where the same people who killed him now revere him as their one and only savior. You need not look further than the person reading the words in this book.

Honestly, if you continue to justify your actions as does every other unique expression of Consciousness, then who is engaging in solely right actions, and who is engaging in exclusively wrong actions? In other words, who do you consider to be a good person, and who is a bad person? The answer is no one person is either. Even me, I am neither solely good nor bad.

You, me, and everyone experiencing Earth life is as good as they are bad. If you recall from your arithmetic teachings, equal opposites cancel one another out and equal to zero, or, in the case of unique expressions of Consciousness, perfect. This is a universal truth! If you disagree, then you must have a justification for why you do. Your justification reinforces the fact that, to Consciousness, you can never do anything wrong. Again, Consciousness does not identify with duality and so does not care about your egoic mind's perceptions of the illusions of right and wrong. So, knock yourself out with your justifications, but don't stay up too late.

Imagine how insane it would be for Consciousness to accept that you incarnate on Earth, where duality exists, expecting that you avoid the unavoidable (unpleasant feelings) in order to save your soul from burning in hell for eternity. Consciousness knows better than to impose this sort of limitation on you. Secondly, for Consciousness to expect this sort of behavior from you would be insane because it would be setting itself up for catastrophic failure and disappointment. Third, this would be entirely unfair to you, as a unique expression of itself.

Why would Consciousness create an experience with options that are enormously stacked against you? These sorts of beliefs are in stark contrast to what an unconditionally loving being would do. Believing that your creator sends only one son to come and save your soul, and the souls of all other beings, is also flawed because many beings will never have the opportunity to know Master Jesus. If that really were the case, then the game, the show, the school, the illusion that is the Earth life experience is entirely rigged, and your creator is not only the opposite of unconditionally loving, but also very unfair.

Your egoic mind might continue to believe this to be the case, but I hope you are beginning to understand all of it to be false. They are false because they arise from your illusionary fear that Consciousness has abandoned you. They are false because they are all illusions.

Because of unconditional love, your eternal salvation is not dependent on anything or anyone other than yourself. Allow me to share another universal truth with you: as you are in your current form and state of consciousness, you are already saved. You are destined for a place much more pleasant than your ideas of what heaven or hell are. You are destined to remember pure bliss, a state of being that transcends duality.

Recap of You Can Do No Wrong

Rule number two governing Earth life, which declares that you are loved unconditionally and have free will to do as your please, implies that, to Consciousness, you can do no wrong, ever.

Consciousness does not identify with dualistic views of right or wrong or good or evil.

Consciousness views all actions that every unique expression of itself engages in as a neutral means to an end. It views the actions as purely blissful. The actions support the expansion of Consciousness.

Your ability to justify your actions is the outcome of your infinitely creative mind's work, and a reflection of your current level of awareness of your connection to Consciousness.

All souls incarnated on Earth justify their actions ceaselessly. Justifying is a means of creative expression. By so doing, no one soul is ever solely right, and none is ever solely wrong. All souls are merely playing their role to expand Consciousness' knowledge of itself.

All unique expressions of Consciousness are as good as they are as bad. The balance means they are always perfect beings in their current state.

Solely by being, you are already saved. Remember, you are a unique expression of Consciousness, and there is nothing and no place outside of Consciousness. You are always connected to Consciousness, even though you might believe otherwise.

Perceived unpleasant actions have the ability to bring unique expressions of Consciousness closer to remembering why they are.

8

Satan, The Devil, is Your Best Friend

"Of all the liars in the world, sometimes the worst are our own fears." —Rudyard Kipling

I f the title of this chapter startles you and makes you think I am anything other than perfect and sane, I can appreciate why you would feel that way. It is your birthright to truly express your honest opinions and feelings always. That said, I want to promise you I am not insane. I intend to show you by the end of this chapter how Satan, the Devil, is indeed your best friend.

You now understand duality's influences on your Earth life experiences. You likely perceive Satan as the most extreme experience and feeling of fear on your duality spectrum. Recall that fears all stem from the false belief or illusion that Consciousness abandoned you to fend for yourself. Because your fears of abandonment are not real, this renders all your fears that arise from this original false belief as not real, either. So, no matter how mild or extreme your fear is, like in the case of Satan, the Devil, none of them are real. Your fears, including your fear of Satan, are misunderstood illusions. They are all illusions, just like the nightmares you experience. This is a universal truth you must become conscious of as you continue to learn why you are.

Similar to understanding that your ego is not real, but it does have an essential role to play while you continue to experience life on Earth, Satan is also not real and also has an essential role to play for you and every other unique expression of Consciousness experiencing life on Earth. Satan's role is no more or less significant than yours in contributing to the grand illusionary Earth show. This is true.

Satan's primary purpose while here on Earth is to bring to life, in convincing fashion, your most creative imaginations of fear. All your fears are your ego's unique and distinct creations; and boy, are you creative. Your fears are tangible proof of this. For that, now is as good a time as ever for me to applaud you for your work. Bravo! Your creative fears are also tangible proof that you are a co-creator of the universe.

See, Satan, just like your ego, really does not exist. They are both necessary illusions that support your ability to experience Earth life. The Satan you believe in is an entirely subjective and unique outcome of your creative imaginations. As a matter of fact, no other unique expression of Consciousness believes in the same Satan. Your Satan is entirely and wholeheartedly yours. Your Satan is a construct of who or what you think is the worst experience of fear you can experience. Your Satan also represents your current level of awareness of your eternal connection to Consciousness. You can test this universal truth by comparing your understandings and beliefs of who or what Satan is to the understandings and beliefs of a close friend or relative. I tried this same experiment with a group of folks while presenting on this topic, and the results were eye-opening for the participants. They were also comical.

To try it for yourself, grab a piece of paper and something to write with. Draw a picture of what you think Satan looks like on the paper. Underneath the picture, write down three words that you believe, without a doubt, are Satan's most telling traits. These are traits that, if anyone used them to describe themselves, would convince you you'd just met Satan. Have your friend or relative do the same. When you are both finished, compare what you each came up with. I am convinced they will differ. I am not trying to incite disagreements between you and your social circle with this exercise, but instead encouraging you to expand your consciousness.

Building on the idea that you and other human beings currently experiencing life on Earth are co-creators of the universe, consider that each one of your fears is your individual creation. Your collective fears are all based on the varying levels of awareness of your individual connections to Consciousness. These fears have no limit, in part because their creators, you and others, are all infinitely creative beings. Although the fears have no limits, the Satan you individually believe in, who is entirely your unique creation, brings them to life in convincing fashion. Satan does this so well that you believe the feelings the fears evoke or the experiences themselves, to be real.

Know that it really isn't Satan bringing the fears to life. You, instead, are the one doing it with your thoughts, actions, and most importantly, with your perceptions. If you continue to think Satan is a separate and real entity and not a construct of your imaginations, please understand then that as a unique expression of Consciousness, Satan remembers his eternal connection to Consciousness. By remembering this connection, he is aware of his infinite creativity, and understands, accepts, and plays his role fully. As a matter of fact, he is playing his role of bringing your fears to life, fearlessly. This means that Satan is living void of fear. Is that not somewhat ironic? The one entity you fear more than anything else actually has no fears! I already alluded to how comical all of Earth life is, and this is another example of it.

The illusionary being you fear so much, Satan, is here on Earth, solely as a construct of your imagination, to bring to life your worst fears. You should be eternally grateful that Satan is versatile enough to bring to life your and all other unique expressions of Consciousness' fears to life, without prejudice. Satan brings your fears to life with as much attention to detail, care, and accountability as he does for everyone else, including your friends and those you despise so much you might wish they never received this kind of premium service, even from Satan.

Satan does this work ceaselessly, every day, regardless of the weather or your current life situation. Satan is as reliable as the sun rising on the eastern horizon every morning. Not that you need a reminder, but realize and appreciate that Satan does this all for free. Satan asks for nothing in return from you when he brings your fears to life in convincing fashion. This is another universal truth.

You likely believe there is a cost for Satan's premium service. You are probably under the impression that Satan is in the business of collecting souls to come and live with him for eternity in hell. Satan is in no such business. Your soul is who you are in your purest and most fundamental form. Your soul is and always will be. Your soul is Consciousness. No one is ever going to buy, sell, or steal your soul, even if you allow it to happen. In my current understanding of the workings of the universe, I do not believe it is possible to sell your soul permanently. Neither you nor anyone else can own what we all are. We are all unique expressions of the same Energy interacting with ourselves. No one and nothing own us.

That said, Satan exists in your mind, and plays his role on Earth for two primary reasons.

Satan Wants to Keep You Safe

The first reason Satan ceaselessly brings your fears to life is because he wants to keep you safe. If this sounds similar to what your ego does for you, indeed it is the case. You should be able to appreciate why this makes sense. Satan is entirely a construct of your ego's creativity. If you (your egoic mind) believe an experience to be one you can categorize on the hellish side of your duality spectrum, or in line with what Satan would want you to do, you do your best to avoid it. By avoiding these Satan-like experiences, your egoic mind believes it is keeping itself safe.

Remember that your egoic mind also attributes feelings of being safe as equivalent to experiences on the heavenly side of your spectrum. What this means is, every time you avoid a Satan-like experience, your egoic mind believes it is experiencing a heaven-like experience. Put another way, your egoic mind attains its heavens by avoiding its hells. In situations where your egoic mind cannot entirely avoid a Satan-like experience, it will find creative alternatives to create a feeling of being safe by surrounding itself with tools (other unique expressions of Consciousness) to help. An example of such a case would be keeping a gun in your house for protection because the house alone does not provide enough security for you to feel safe.

You do this for all your fears, including those that you are not aware of, regardless of how mild or extreme you choose to categorize them on your duality spectrum. For as long as you continue to experience Earth life under the illusion that Consciousness has abandoned you, you will continue to avoid your hells and seek your heavens. Here is another universal truth to understand about this dance you partake in, which I introduced in the previous chapter.

So long as you are on Earth living in fear, no experience is solely what you perceive it to be. No heavenly experience of yours is solely heavenly, just like no hellish experience is solely hellish. All your experiences are simultaneously both, always and forever. This further explains the balance of Consciousness and rule number one that governs all the universe, including Earth life experiences.

As you continue to live under the illusion that Consciousness has abandoned you, every heaven you attain on Earth will simultaneously create a hell you need to contend with. Similarly, every hell you experience will leave you longing for a heaven to experience as well. Review the story of Master Jesus and the mob to learn more about this reality of the Earth life experience. It truly is an unavoidable reality, and you knew this before deciding to partake in the game; before enrolling in the school; before auditioning to play a role in the show. Again, this is testament to the fact that you are a brave soul. As an aside, the idea that no experience is solely a heavenly or hellish experience should make you think more about the saying, *Be careful what you wish for.*

Consider the following example demonstrating how Satan works to help keep you safe:

Imagine that you continue to live under the illusion that Consciousness has abandoned you and are, therefore, still living in fear. Imagine that to help you feel safe and maintain a sense of community, you decide to get a dog as a companion pet. The interesting thing about your deciding to get a dog is this: you live in a community where eating dog meat is not an issue for most of the community members. As a matter of fact, you have eaten some dog meat in the recent past, but after the last time you ate dog meat, you had an interesting dream. The dog's soul visited you in your dream and expressed to you all the pain and anguish it experienced because you killed it, cooked it, and ate it. It did not stop there, and promised to haunt you in your dreams every single night until you remedied the situation by rescuing a dog and raising it as a loving member of your family. Mind you, you live in a community where eating dog meat is normal. I should also add that treating and loving dogs as members of the family is not normal in this community. You would be an outlier in the community if you began to show dogs this kind of love and attention. What would you do?

Consider all the possible fears that your creative mind would create in the example presented above. Maybe one of the fears is not being able to sleep through the night because of the promise of haunting dreams from a dog you just ate. Lack of sleep means your job will suffer, which means your ability to provide for your family will also suffer. You might even be thinking, *There goes my ability to have enough money to purchase dog meat ever again.*

Alternatively, you might be worried about being ridiculed within the community by members who discover you being loving and caring to dogs. You might be anxious about your ability to protect the dog from community members who want to eat it. Besides that, you might be worried about your ability to love a dog. What would your immediate family think if they saw you showing as much love and affection to a dog as you did to them? These are just a few examples of the fears your mind can create given the situation. The number of fears your mind can create are endless. What other fears can you think of experiencing in this scenario that Satan could bring to life for you?

For the sake of proving my point that Satan is your friend because he wants to keep you safe, and of wanting to keep things simple, let us assume that you decide not to rescue a dog. Instead, you decide that you will never again eat dog meat in any capacity. You convince yourself that this decision is as good a decision as any you can come up with, and it is a fair remedy for your previous behaviors. Since you convince yourself that this decision is a good one, it helps you feel safe. Realize what Satan has done for you here. Satan has brought your fears to life in so convincing a fashion that you believed them to be real. Satan showed you your fears of a dead dog's soul hunting you every night, and by so doing, required you to seek a feeling of safety. Realize that you created your safe feeling by deciding and convincing yourself that not eating dog meat ever again was good enough. You believe that not eating dog meat will keep the dead dog's soul away from you and out of your dreams.

I need you to appreciate how this new belief that you created, along with the many other beliefs that you hold, only appear to protect you from the illusions of fear you create that Satan brings to life. The feelings of safety, however, are also only temporary. Consider in the above example how, even though you have decided not to eat dog meat any longer, the fear of ridicule and embarrassment you might experience from your community members will still be a feeling you have to contend with. You might be further fearful of your ability to keep your promise of never again eating dog meat. Alternatively, since not eating dog meat was not what the dead dog's soul requested of you, the idea of the dog still haunting your dreams could be another source of fear.

So, as you become appreciative of how Satan brings your fears to life in convincing fashion to help keep you safe, please appreciate how you can never truly be safe. While experiencing life on Earth, and still living under the illusion of fear of Consciousness abandoning you, safe feelings are only temporary, just like hellish feelings are also only temporary. The feelings are temporary because of duality's influence on rule number one (the balance of Consciousness). In truth, all earthly experiences are just as good as they are bad. While you are experiencing heaven by not eating dog meat, you will still have a hell to contend with.

Now consider that it has been five years since you decided to stop eating dog meat in any capacity, and that you have succeeded in keeping the promise. Today, not only do you no longer eat dog meat, you are also not bothered by the thought of anyone else eating dog meat. Your feelings toward this issue are entirely neutral. When I say your feelings are neutral, I mean they make you neither happy nor sad. You would place your perception of such an experience right in the middle of your duality spectrum.

In other words, you perceive the experience as just as good as it is bad, and neither good nor bad.

If you do possess this type of perception towards this or any such experience, please recognize in this moment that it is a perfect indication of you living in bliss. Living in bliss is living void of fears or desires. By not having any desires to eat dog meat or to stop anyone else from eating dog meat, and not fearing the consequences, you are living in state of no desires or fears. This is what I refer to as living in a state of bliss. See, it is no fairy tale.

I hope this demonstrates how much of a friend Satan is to you. Satan cares so deeply about you that he works ceaselessly every day to bring to life your fears in convincing fashion. Satan does this so you can employ your infinite creativity to come up with solutions that keep you safe. Of course, this is not the only reason why Satan is a friend of yours.

Satan Wants You to Remember the Real You

The second reason Satan ceaselessly brings your fears to life in convincing fashion is because Satan understands that doing so helps you remember who you truly are. Satan wants nothing more than for you to stop identifying with the illusionary you, your ego, and to remember who you are in your purest and most fundamental essence, Consciousness. This sounds counter-intuitive, but it is true.

As you continue to live in fear by believing the illusion that Consciousness has abandoned you, you will ceaselessly identify fears in your earthly experiences and create solutions to keep you safe from them. You are now aware that no feeling of safety you create is permanent, and eventually introduces a fear for you to contend with. Imagine that you perform this back-and-forth dance over numerous lifetimes. The more and more fears you create, and the more solutions you create for the fears, the more you augment the illusion of being separate from Consciousness. Eventually, you will reach a point when you will have stretched the illusion so far that even your egoic mind will begin to question why it can never be satisfied in its current state of being. This realization is the catalyst for you to begin asking the right questions to help you remember who and why you are.

Everyone experiences this remembrance in their death. Others may experience a traumatic event in their life that causes them to begin to seek bliss and peace outside of their earthly reality. Some are lucky enough they do not have to experience death to begin to ask these questions. In my case, I am grateful I did not have to experience such a traumatic event.

Now, why Satan wants you to remember who you truly are is important. Once you remember who you are, you remember, amongst other things, that you are infinitely creative (just like Satan). This means you can identify the most complex fears and create the most complex solutions to counterbalance the fears. The complex fears that you create from this new state of being are not fears, but instead byproducts of your attempts at expressing your infinite creativity to create whatever you think is possible.

This new perspective of yours bodes well for Satan. As you flex your infinite creativity muscles, these complex fears, or rather, complex expressions of possibilities keep Satan busy; they keep Satan employed. They provide tremendous opportunity for Satan to improve the skills and abilities he employs to bring them to life. Surely you can understand that Satan must continuously improve his skills or else he will be rusty at his job. Besides, I am certain you agree that unemployment is an unpleasant state of being for anyone, especially someone who provides premium services at no cost. Satan loves his job and would love nothing more than for you to remember who you truly are. Even if you don't, Satan still provides premium services for you with no prejudice.

Before finally understanding that Satan is my best friend and entirely a creative construct of my mind, I also feared him. I believed he was out for my soul and was gaining a foothold of it every time my actions were unpleasant. When I began meditating, I experienced kriyas. Kriyas are involuntary body movements. I discuss them more in Chapter 14. I introduce them here to let you know that, because of my false beliefs of Satan, I thought kriyas were a representation of Satan's possession of me. It was only after my awakening that I began to see Satan for who he really is. Since then, my relationship with him has been nothing but beneficial. I now believe Satan really wanted me to remember who I truly was. Experiencing Earth life from the perspective of knowing who I truly am means my desires no longer come from a space of fear, but from one of possibilities. Consider the following example below to understand this.

After remembering these universal truths, I thought to share them with the world. One way to accomplish this was to write a book. I had never written a book before and had no idea how to begin. Early in the process, I identified with this knowledge and these thoughts as fears, which Satan gladly brought to life for me in convincing fashion. What if I didn't have enough time to write the book? What if I couldn't find a publisher? What if I couldn't find an editor willing to work with me? What if I didn't have enough money to get the book published? What if I didn't sell enough copies of my book? These are just a few of the many fears I identified with, which Satan made sure I was convinced were real.

When I noticed what Satan was doing for me, I smiled. I thought to myself, *If another unique expression of Consciousness has published a book while dealing with the same or similar fears that their Satan brought to life for them, it is entirely possible for me to publish a book, too.* Working from this space of possibility, I realized how my Satan was instead showing me what I needed to focus on to reach my goal. Satan was indirectly encouraging me to find creative solutions to do what was possible. It was due to Satan's work that I identified possible solutions to ensure this book got published.

Take, for example, Satan bringing to life the thought that I would not find an editor willing to work with me. From a space of possibility, I realized Satan was showing me that I needed an editor to help me elevate how I presented the messages in this book. After becoming aware of this, I also understood it was entirely possible to find an editor. Working with this knowledge and from a space of possibility, I connected with an editor who was more than willing and excited to work with me on my book. Not only that, our schedules worked out perfectly for when we could begin to collaborate, which was no coincidence, either.

As you can see from my personal experience, by bringing your fears to life in convincing fashion, Satan is prompting you to remember who you truly are. That way, you can begin to live from a space of infinite possibilities and create solutions to overcome your fears. Satan does his job so that you can begin to understand that your fears are your own creative mind's constructs. In other words, so that you can perceive your fears as illusionary and necessary opportunities to express your creativity. Satan works with you so you can remember that the fears you create and solutions you create all help Consciousness expand knowledge of itself. This is also precisely why you are.

Why You Should Overcome Your Fears

I am confident you would agree that overcoming your fears evokes an emotion of delight within you. If you can think back to a time when you overcame a fear and imagine how you felt, you would find this to be true. Overcoming your fears adds fuel to the flickering flame of belief you possess of possibly being capable of doing more than you imagine. The more you overcome fears and experience this feeling, the more it helps the flickering flame burn as a steady, bright, eternally burning fire of belief in your ability to achieve unlimited possibilities.

It not only opens the floodgates and frees your infinite creativity, as you have seen, but it also helps you remember your eternal connection to Consciousness.

Satan, your best friend and the construct of your own creative mind, wishes nothing more for you than that you continue to overcome your fears. That is why he works tirelessly to present you your fears in convincing fashion.

Hell on Earth

At this time, you may be wondering what happens if Satan brings your fears to life and you do not overcome them. Or what happens if you do not even recognize them and, therefore, would not have the opportunity to overcome them. Or what happens if you recognize them but choose not to overcome them.

Never worry that Satan wins and gains control of your soul if you fail to overcome a fear he brings to life for you. If you continue to think this way, it means you continue to live under the illusion that Consciousness has abandoned you. You are not wrong for thinking this way, but it is not what happens.

If you fail to overcome your fears after Satan presents them to you, Satan will not give up. Remember that Satan is a reliable friend who cares deeply about you and wants nothing more than for you to overcome your fears. Satan is also a being who remembers his eternal connection to Consciousness, which means that he is infinitely creative. What this means is Satan will leverage his infinite creativity to ceaselessly present your fears to you until you eventually overcome them. Satan will present the fears to you through myriad experiences, scenarios, and life situations. Though the experiences, scenarios, and life situations will likely change, the fear that you need to be aware of and overcome will stay the same.

Take one of my experiences as an example. At the time of this writing, I worked as the pharmacy director at a critical access hospital in a beautiful rural town. I was younger than some of the pharmacists who reported to me. This made me feel nervous and uncomfortable when I needed to have tough conversations about their performance being below the hospital's employee standards. When opportunities would arise to have tough conversations, my initial solution was to avoid them and hope the pharmacist would find intrinsic reasons to improve their behaviors. Alternatively, I hoped and convinced myself that the incidences were isolated, and that the situations would work themselves out.

The more I avoided having the conversations, the more the opportunities to have the conversations presented themselves. I even began to receive complaints from other managers about my staff, which is never an easy situation to be in as a department head. Eventually, I found myself in a position where I could no longer avoid my fears of holding tough conversations with employees who were older than me. I had to face them. I will have you know, it was only after facing the fear that I became comfortable holding tough conversations with my coworkers. In fact, after my first tough conversation, I realized my imaginations of the experience were worse than the actual experience.

All our actions, regardless of what they are, are teaching all of Consciousness more and more about itself. You do not even have to intend for this to happen, and they will still provide teaching and learning opportunities. Realize how my coworker exhibiting behavior that was not representative of the hospital's employee standards eventually led to my identifying my fear of holding tough conversations. My Satan brought the fear to life in convincing fashion for me, and I worked to overcome it. I am sure my coworker never purposefully and consciously acted the way they did, thinking it would help me overcome my fears. Not at all. Instead, they were just being themselves, expressing how they truly felt about the situation they were in.

Back to experiencing hell on Earth: if not at your job, Satan could present fears to you through a recurring dream, or by helping you recognize how your previous seven romantic partners all had similar personality traits. An even more interesting method Satan could employ to reveal your fears to you could be helping you realize your perceptions of your Earth life experiences. You may find that you cannot tolerate or maintain any semblance of a relationship with anyone in your social or professional circle, even though they are all individuals from varying backgrounds. Money is another excellent avenue for Satan to reveal your fears to you. If you fear that you do not have enough money to do something, then you will not have enough money to.

The point is, there are myriad methods Satan employs to present you your fears. What is more important than realizing this is that you pay attention to your earthly experiences and recognize the repeating patterns in your life. These repeating patterns are your fears Satan is presenting to you. After you recognize the fears, work diligently to overcome them.

Remember, though, that Consciousness loves you unconditionally and has also granted you free will to do as you please. By exercising your free will, you may choose to overcome your fears once you realize them. So long as you continue to live under the illusion of abandonment, overcoming any of your fears will only create another one for you to overcome later.

Alternatively, you may employ your free will to continue holding onto the fear for whatever reason of your choosing. Understand that doing so means you will continue living with the fear, and Satan, your friend, will continue presenting the fear to you for the duration of your current Earth life. What results is, your Earth life becomes an endlessly recurring pattern in which you experience the same fears over and over and over. Reliving a recurring pattern sounds both insane and like the most horrific thing you can experience. It describes another one of your worst fears—your fear of living in Hell for eternity.

From reading the Bible or through some other avenue you have come across in your current Earth life, you may have heard and come to believe that Hell is a place where you burn for eternity but never die. Alternatively, you may have come to believe that Hell is a place where you develop an eternal thirst that no amount of water, or beverage of your choice, can quench. These descriptions of Hell are metaphors for what I just described. This is another universal truth I am sharing with you now.

Your best friend, Satan—sorry, I mean your own creative mind—will continue to present you your fears throughout your earthly incarnation in your various experiences until you acknowledge and overcome them. Not overcoming them and continuing to relive the fear in perpetuity is the textbook definition of living in Hell. This is true. Hell is not a place you go to burn for eternity after you die. Like Satan, Hell is entirely a construct of your infinitely creative mind.

You have every right not to believe me or overcome any of your fears, and instead, to choose to continue reliving the same fears every day of your life until you die. It makes me wonder why you, or anyone for that matter, would accept to maintain such a lifestyle? I mean, you can get out of Hell by overcoming the fears that you create for yourself, starting this very instant. If you are so fearful of the idea of living in Hell for eternity after you die, why do you continue to live in Hell while on Earth? It makes no sense to me.

If both Hell and Satan are creative constructs of your mind, I hope this realization makes you wonder who or what God is? If that's the case, terrific. Allow me to explain.

Your God is Your Satan

I have done my best to avoid using the word God thus far in my writing for an important reason. Your idea of God, just like that of

Satan, is entirely a construct of your egoic mind. Your God is a product of you exercising your infinite creativity and attempting to make sense of your Earth life experiences. Since God is a product of your egoic mind, your idea of God is limited by your understanding of the workings of the universe, and by the level of awareness you possess of your connection to Consciousness. Your idea of God is an illusionary vision of what your ultimate experience of safety and belonging is. Your God epitomizes your beliefs of living void of fears.

Just like your idea of who or what Satan is, is uniquely yours, so too is your idea of who or what your belief of God is. It is entirely subjective. I can appreciate that reading about God being a construct of your mind may be difficult and even blasphemous to hear, but I want to assure you that it is a universal truth. Now is also a good time to remind you of rule number two governing all of Earth life. It is your right to believe this to be true or not.

Truthfully, your ideas of both God and Satan are based entirely on your fears and beliefs and represent the extreme ends of your duality spectrum. Before I remembered my eternal connection to Consciousness, I also created and believed ideas of who and what I thought God and Satan were. It is a necessary part of experiencing Earth life, as the ideas help provide meaning to our experiences. You may also appreciate my admitting that my understanding of who God and Satan were changed frequently based on my Earth life situation. Maybe you may find some resonance in knowing that the God you currently believe in is not the same God you believed in as a child, or last year, or maybe even last month. Neither is the Satan that you currently fear the same one you feared at some point in the past.

Please recognize how your mind changes who both God and Satan are as your awareness of your Connection to Consciousness changes. This will continue to happen as long as you continue to live in fear. Never forget that, regardless of what concepts your egoic mind creates about who and what both God and Satan are, Consciousness will always love you unconditionally. You are on your unique path to eventually remembering who you are in your purest essence, and every experience and belief that you create is helping you along your journey.

To continue to fully understand why you are, it is necessary for you to recognize the universal truth that both God and Satan are illusions, just like your ego is. As illusions, they are essential to helping you survive your Earth life experience, and that is it. Even more shocking than the idea of God and Satan being illusions is the universal truth that they are two sides of the same being.

The God that you love and pray to in times of despair is the Satan you fear, loathe, and try to avoid like the plague. They both represent the extreme ends of your duality spectrum. They are both your ego's attempt at understanding Consciousness' ceaseless desire to create and change.

Remember that no person, thing, or experience on Earth is immune to duality. Even your ego is not immune to duality. Your ego is as good as it is evil; your ego is equally God and Satan. This is true. God and Satan are virtually inseparable. Just like you cannot separate the head from the tail of a coin, you cannot separate your creative constructs of God and Satan. I'll repeat that they are actually your ego's attempt at understanding Consciousness' ceaseless desire to create and change.

If you continue to believe that God and Satan are not entirely constructs of your mind, then maybe you can begin to appreciate that both are also unique expressions of Consciousness. Naturally then, because you believe they have tremendous creative powers, you can appreciate that they also remember their eternal connection to Consciousness, and both, therefore, experience Earth life void of the fear of abandonment. You are already very familiar with Satan's essential role for you while you continue to experience Earth life. As Satan shows you what your fears are so you can avoid or overcome them, God shows you what it feels like to experience being safe from your fears by avoiding and overcoming them.

It is a wonderfully designed and symbiotic relationship. Know that Satan's greatest desires and wishes for you are no different from God's greatest desires and wishes for you. They both want you to remember who you are in your purest essence. They are both performing their roles so reliably and with love, care, and compassion so that you quickly remember you are Consciousness.

Naturally, this bodes well for God because when you remember, your creative solutions are more complex. The more complex solutions ensure that God is not out of a job, and also that he continues to improve his ability to bring your experiences of Heaven to life in convincing fashion. Additionally, both God and Satan know that after you remember you are Consciousness, you begin to experience Earth life from a state of bliss.

What Exactly is This Bliss I Keep Mentioning?

You must understand that living in bliss on Earth means living from the same perspective as *You* do. It means understanding that you are not separate or alone, and that you are eternally connected to everything in the entire cosmos. It means understanding that you are loved unconditionally and have free will to do as you please. It means accepting your limitless self.

Living in bliss means living from a state of being that transcends duality. This state of being transcends the notions of good and evil and right and wrong, and of God and Satan. It requires understanding and accepting that every experience is no more than a neutral means to end for Consciousness. It is understanding that every experience is both a lesson and a blessing.

Living in bliss requires that you understand, accept, and experience God and Satan as two sides of the same being who cannot be separated. Living in bliss means appreciating God's and Satan's role as essential parts of the illusion that is life on Earth, and naturally becoming comfortable working with both to ensure your personal growth.

Living in bliss means coming to terms with the knowledge that Satan is not only the other side of God, but he is also your friend. Living in bliss means accepting that, as your friend, Satan not only cares about keeping you safe, but he also supports your growth towards remembering who you truly are. Both God and Satan support your growth by allowing you to take the illusion of abandonment to the extreme and to stretch your creative muscles to come up with your worst fears and greatest joys.

Living in bliss means appreciating God's and Satan's reliability and versatility, as you can always trust both to bring your fears and joys to life in convincing fashion. Living in bliss means believing God and Satan love it when you overcome your fears—just as much as, if not more than, Satan loves bringing them to life for you. Living in bliss means never forgetting that both Satan and God rejoice when you remember your eternal connection to Consciousness and return home. It is a beautiful thing when you do.

The Bible story of the prodigal son is a metaphor describing when this happens. There is a great celebration throughout all of Consciousness when a unique expression of itself returns home.

And finally, living in bliss means understanding, knowing, and accepting that both God and Satan are your egoic mind's own creative expression. They are not real. Only the real you, your soul, which is pure Consciousness, is real. You, as your ego, are a temporary illusion working to help Consciousness expand knowledge of itself.

Now that you understand what bliss is, do me a favor. Become familiar with every aspect of your life that you believe Satan and God helped shape. You now know they will always be present in your Earth life as products of your mind, so learning to work with them is important. As you become increasingly comfortable working with both, you will begin to gain control of your mind, and you will slowly begin to create the Earth life experience you wish for yourself.

Both God and Satan understand this and are playing their roles perfectly for you so that you do not fail; you cannot fail. At all times, grant both God and Satan permission to help you remember who and why you truly are and your eternal connection to Consciousness. As you work with them, you will grow further into your infinitely creative self. Again, you cannot fail, and as rule number two explained, Consciousness will love you unconditionally for eternity.

God and Satan are two sides of the same being who want nothing but the best for you. Because they are entirely illusionary creations of your egoic mind, you are essentially God and Satan, and want nothing but the best for yourself. You are your best friend.

Recap of Satan, The Devil, is Your Best Friend

Satan is an illusionary and subjective construct of an illusion, your ego.

Satan represents your ego's misunderstood and ceaseless desires of Consciousness to 'change.'

Satan represents the extreme end of the unpleasant side of your duality spectrum.

Satan's role on Earth is to bring your most creative fears to life in convincing fashion. He does this reliably and always.

Working with Satan helps your overcome your fears, which helps you remember who you are, and why you are. Your work inevitably helps Consciousness expand knowledge of itself, too.

Satan, being a product of your egoic mind, and one end of your duality spectrum, is the other side of the God you believe in.

Since both God and Satan are illusions of your mind, you are essentially both the God and Satan your mind creates.

9

Your Beliefs Limit You

"We see the world not as it is but as we are." —Talmud

You can appreciate your egoic mind and its infinitely creative ability to identify fears, create solutions to those fears, and hold onto the solutions as beliefs. You may also appreciate that those solutions or beliefs become your habits. These habits define the character you are currently playing as you experience life on Earth. They define how members of your social circle perceive you, and, to an extent, how you wish members of your social circle perceived you (what is your reality versus what you wish was your reality).

Your beliefs also define you by being the guidepost or compass that direct you to avoid experiences you would categorize as unpleasant, and to seek those you would categorize as pleasant. In other words, your beliefs shape your duality spectrum, and your duality spectrum limits you. You create many of these beliefs for yourself as you continue to experience different facets of Earth life, and for many other beliefs, you accept them to be true because you convince yourself that they can provide you safety. You do this either consciously or unconsciously all the time.

Regardless of whether you created or accepted the beliefs, you must know that every single one of them originates from the same fear that caused you to create your ego: that you are all alone because Consciousness has abandoned you for some reason. Also, you must know that every belief is not only limiting you to pleasant experiences, but also affecting your perceptions of all your illusionary Earth life experiences. In other words, what you believe is what you perceive in the world, and what you perceive in the world is your truth.

Your beliefs are your truth and yours only, and they reflect your current level of awareness of your connection to Consciousness. Your beliefs, your truths, represent how much you know about who and why you truly are. Never forget that no belief or truth of yours is right, just as none is wrong. They simply are a means to an end for you, to justify your current actions or behaviors. Since they originate from your egoic mind, they are also temporary illusionary opportunities to express your infinite creativity, which helps Consciousness expand. Naturally, because this is precisely why you are.

To illustrate this universal truth that your beliefs are infinitely creative and temporary expressions (justifications) of who you believe you are in the moment, consider the following example.

You and your two-year-old niece are playing with plastic letters of the alphabet and numbers. By playing with her, you are helping her expand her Consciousness, you lovely soul, and that is mighty sweet of you.

At some point, you pick the alphabet piece that looks like a zero and call it the letter *O*. Your niece immediately changes the expressions on her face. She goes from calm and jovial to bewildered and confused, and just as quickly, to confident and aware. She looks at you and adamantly tells you that you are wrong. She further explains that it is not the letter *O*, it is the number zero.

At that, you smile in your heart. You know your niece's knowledge of numbers and letters is still developing and you think it is cute that she believes you were wrong. You may experience bliss in the moment. You realize you do not have to belittle your niece and make her feel bad for mistaking a letter and a number—no. You could choose to explain to her why they are different, or you could appreciate that she will inevitably come to know the difference one day and go on from there.

This simple example illustrates the universal truth that your beliefs are creative justification opportunities to express your current level of awareness of your connection to Consciousness. They also illustrate how your beliefs create the world that you experience by limiting your perceptions. Since your niece believed the letter *O* to be the number zero, in her world, you were incorrect and needed to be corrected. In your world, she was a child still learning the differences, and was neither right nor wrong. She was cute in her misunderstanding.

I remind you of the limitations of your beliefs because it is necessary to understand in order to remember why your Earth life is the way it is. Particularly, it is important that you become cognizant of the universal truth that all your beliefs stem from the illusionary fear that Consciousness abandoned you.

I invite you to spend time investigating why you hold on to your current beliefs and become familiar with the fear-like experiences that caused you to create or accept them. You may even choose to investigate the laws that govern our societies and the beliefs that many different religious organizations ascribe to, and you will arrive at the same conclusion. They all originate from a desire to protect the egoic self.

One example of such a belief was the one I learned through my Catholic teachings. The belief taught me to deal with the guilt of experiencing financial success while many people suffered in the world by donating at least ten percent of my earnings to the church or charitable organization. Simple beliefs like this limit the perceptions of our Earth life experiences.

By the way, my mentioning of governments, religious organizations, or businesses using your fears to sell you solutions as products or services is in no way suggesting that they are right or wrong to do so. Remember, they are all unique expressions of Consciousness, just like you, and are also subject to the same two rules governing life on Earth. Because of rule one, they are a necessary part of maintaining the balance. And because of rule two, they have as much right to free will and unconditional love as you do. What you must accept is that you are the sole actor and the director of your Earth life show, with full authority and responsibility to decide to ascribe to or reject the fears and solutions that they present to you. I expand on this notion of being the actor and the director of your Earth life show in Chapter 10.

Your Beliefs Give Birth to Your Habits

It is additionally important to pay attention to your habits. Your habits are a result of continuing to live your life under the guidance of your fear-based beliefs. Your habits represent your egoic mind's attempt to keep you safe. Your habits are repetitive behaviors and actions that you believe will help you avoid fear in your experiences. You may not be fully aware of your habits and how they limit you from experiencing the Earth life you wish for yourself. What I mean is, you may be struggling to attain a goal that you fail to realize is impossible because one of your fear-based beliefs has caused you to develop a habit that defines and confines you.

Until you are comfortable enough learning what the belief is, acknowledging the fear that caused you to create it, and then letting go of the fear, you will struggle to change the habit or attain your Earth life visions.

It is no different from trying to clean your floor with dirty water. You can spend eternity changing the bucket and the mop, but will never attain a clean floor if you do not change the water. The water is a metaphor for your beliefs. The mop and bucket are your habits. Appreciate how changing your habits will produce a temporary, slightly better result; however, changing your beliefs will result in a more lasting and improved outcome, and does not require that you necessarily change your habits—though they, too, will likely change.

Duality and Its Effects on Your Beliefs

As far as the concept of duality and its effects on your beliefs, appreciate how they feed off each other to keep you living in fear and creating safe beliefs in perpetuity. Remember that no experience is solely good or evil, and your perception of what any experience is reflects who you believe you are in the moment. And because no perception of fear or safety that you experience is permanent, you have no choice but to continue to build on either.

All your fears cause you to create solutions that keep you safe. If the solution is successful, the thoughts that generated the action becomes your beliefs temporarily. Over time, you will no longer perceive the solutions/beliefs as capable of keeping you safe, and you will create more complex beliefs to protect you from the new fears.

Your Earthly desires are an excellent illustration of the symbiotic relationship between beliefs and duality. Because you continue to live in fear, you are unable to find bliss in your experiences or current life situation, even when the experiences represent what you wished for.

You might want a job and believe the job will make you happy and cause you to find peace. You may even say things like, "If only I could get a job doing _____, my life would be perfect." After getting the job, your life is perfect only temporarily before you begin to find reasons why your co-workers, your job, and your boss are the picture-perfect reflections of what you do not need in your life. This is classic fear-based living behavior. It is quite comical, too, but you already know this, as you have come to accept that the Earth life experience is a comedy in its own right.

By the way, are you beginning to see the connection between this back-and-forth dance and being a unique expression of Consciousness? Are you beginning to become aware of your ceaseless desires to continue building on your Earth life experiences by creating and changing your beliefs and fears? I certainly hope so. It is a fundamental characteristic of being *You*. It is precisely why you are. Anyway, I digress.

Geography Influences your Beliefs, Which Limits You, Too

Where you grew up on the planet, and the environmental elements that were present while you grew up, have also had a profound impact on your beliefs. Your community's collective fears and beliefs were the basis for the beliefs you subscribed to in your early years, and for those you later created for yourself. The schools, churches, jobs, and social events you experienced all had some role to play in crafting the beliefs you currently hold.

These beliefs are what you may consider to be the norms and traditions of a group of people that inhabit an area. They are the reasons for the beautiful, rich, and diverse cultures we have across the planet and throughout the cosmos. Languages are a beautiful example of how beliefs, norms, and traditions based on geographical locations allow you to express your infinite creativity. They help keep you safe and simultaneously limit you.

Consider how limiting Mandarin is for someone who can communicate only in Mandarin but is stranded in a German airport on a layover. Other noteworthy examples of how environmentally derived beliefs, norms, and traditions are limiting your perceptions to either being pleasant or unpleasant include the perceptions you develop towards the myriad types of foods available in different cultures, and the methods employed to prepare them in the cultures across the globe. For example, would you eat raw or cooked monkey brain?

Seasonal Beliefs

Rule number two grants you full rights to create and change your beliefs whenever you feel like. Consciousness understands that creating and changing your beliefs is no more than a neutral means to an end for you, as you continue to attempt to keep yourself safe. Remember, you can do no wrong in anything you do, including and especially modifying your beliefs. You have done so your entire life, either consciously or unconsciously. The proof of it is your current life situation, including your social circle and all your possessions.

Your entire life situation is a product of your vision of what is and should be, your beliefs that you can either achieve or fail to achieve it, the actions you engaged in to achieve them, and how you perceive your earthly experiences. Everything about your current life originated from a thought you had and the belief that you can manifest it. As you are able to manifest your current life situation, you can change your beliefs at any time to change your life situation into one you wish to experience. This is a universal truth.

You are an infinitely creative being, and thinking you are anything but, severely limits you. Nothing and no one should limit you, as there is nothing you cannot create in the physical world that you can think of in your mind. Everything is available to you that you will ever need to create anything you can imagine, right away when you wake up from sleep in the morning and until and through the night as you sleep. If you can imagine it and believe in your ability to experience or create it, you can manifest it. Only your fears limit the endless possibilities available to you to achieve your greatest dreams and desires. This is another universal truth.

Consider this example that illustrates how you may change your beliefs without fully understanding that changing your beliefs changes the world you experience and how you act in it.

Imagine that, as a three-year-old, you ask your uncle, who is babysitting you, where babies come from. You can appreciate that because of a host of fears your uncle possesses, he provides you with an answer to your question that is not entirely the reality of where babies come from. One of the fears may be the amount of trouble (uncle's perception of the reaction) he would face from your mom if she found out that he told you, in fine detail, where babies come from. To avoid the start of World War III, he may tell you that a stork delivers babies. Or that babies come from your mother's stomach, and they get there from her eating a ton of food.

Realize how his solution to his fear is to do whatever he can to protect both himself and you. His solution is a means to an end for him. Whether you believe it is right or wrong for your uncle to lie to the three-year-old you, right or wrong for him to avoid telling that version of you the full truth, or right or wrong for him not to even attempt to answer the question is also a means to an end for you. Now, because you are on Earth, this solution that your uncle perceives to protect both you and him is only going to do so for a short while—it is a temporary safe feeling.

In your teenage years, your consciousness would have expanded enough for you to appreciate that having sex is the catalyst for making babies. With this newfound understanding, you may think back to what your uncle told you and wonder why he never explained the truth. You may think and accept that he did not tell you the truth because he believed you would not understand it. Whatever justification you create for why your uncle avoided telling you the truth is also nothing more than a means to an end for you to feel safe.

After learning where babies come from and how to make them, you may perceive the idea of having sex with boys as entirely disgusting and gross, because of course, boys have cooties, are uncivilized, and whatever else. So, you decide you want nothing to do with boys and avoid them like the plague. Appreciate how, because you develop and accept this belief, your interactions with boys are conservative and limiting, and that they simultaneously make you feel safe.

Fast-forward another ten years after you have had many experiences and opportunities to expand your consciousness. With this newfound perspective, you now accept that boys are a necessary part of helping you attain your vision of becoming a mother. The idea of interacting with boys or having sex switches from the unpleasant side to the pleasant side of your duality spectrum. In other words, you change your beliefs to reflect this new desire of yours.

I hope you can appreciate how after changing your beliefs, your habits and perception of your Earth life situation begins to change also. You may begin to present yourself to the world in a manner you believe will attract the type of mate you would love to be a father to your future kids. Lucky for you, things go well, and you marry this person. The idea of having sex, which you initially perceived as unpleasant, becomes a necessary pleasantry for you as you attempt to have your first baby. Heck, you may enjoy the experience so much that you end up having multiple babies of your own. Funnily enough, your uncle, who was fearful and reluctant to tell you where babies came from earlier in your life, will now be celebrating with you every time you give birth. What the what!?

I tell you, if you can appreciate the lessons in the example above, you are closer than you have ever been to remembering who and why you truly are. Notice how both you and your uncle changed your beliefs when you felt they would keep you safe. You changed your beliefs when you felt they would help you attain the type of Earth life vision you wished to experience for yourself. You changed them without thinking much about whether they were right or wrong. Instead, you changed them because doing so was a necessary means to an end for you.

Also, notice how your beliefs always reflected your current level of awareness of your connection to Consciousness. As your consciousness expanded, so did your beliefs. Notice how after changing and adopting the new beliefs, you changed how you acted in your Earth life. Deciding that you were ready to be a mother also meant engaging in the act of having sex. Not only that, I need you to also notice how everything you needed to help you feel safe, or to help you attain the vision of the Earth life experience you wished for yourself, was readily available to you. Notice how your fears and not any other person's fears limited you, and your uncle's fears limited him. And finally, notice how your beliefs, as illusionary solutions to your illusionary fears, are not permanent, either. They are seasonal.

Considering that Consciousness does not identify with duality, I hope you now understand that neither you nor your uncle did anything wrong in the above example. Instead, remember that your actions are always subject to rule number one governing Earth life, and will result in an equal and opposite reaction. Both your actions and the subsequent opposite reactions are a means to an end for you and some other unique expression of Consciousness. If you continue to live in fear, you may identify this balance as an unpleasant experience and allow it to prevent you from attaining your desires. The truth is, no matter what you do, you cannot avoid the balancing act.

As every unique expression of Consciousness on Earth, including you, is ceaselessly working towards attaining a desire, your actions represent indirect reactions to other unique expressions of Consciousness' actions, and vice versa. Put another way, your gains represent losses for others, just like your losses represent gains for others. There really aren't losses or gains, because all of Consciousness gains by expanding its knowledge of itself. When you are indifferent about gaining or losing and only focused on attaining your end, your actions represent your means, the same way Consciousness perceives them—in a non-dual, neither right nor wrong, but rather neutral manner.

To further expand your consciousness and understanding of who and why you truly are, refer to the example above, and reflect on the following questions. Do you, based on your beliefs, norms, and morals think the God you believe in thought your uncle not telling you the whole truth was right or wrong? Or that you not telling your niece the difference between the number zero and letter *O* was right or wrong? Do you think your God will use this and similar actions of yours to judge you and decide to either grant your soul access to Heaven or condemn it to burn in Hell for eternity? Lastly, based on your beliefs, norms and morals, do you think your God thought it was right or wrong for you to initially think making babies was disgusting and then later decide to have many of your own? Regardless of how you answer, I hope you do not answer by saying something along the lines of, "Because Master Jesus is my savior, I am saved from my actions."

Even Science is Limited by Beliefs

Science is also a source of fascination for me and has been so throughout my life. I must acknowledge the myriad societal benefits that we enjoy as a result of scientific studies and discoveries. I am a pharmacist myself, so you can appreciate that my education involved many years studying science-based subjects. To me, science is no different from religion in that they both have a set of beliefs that govern their understandings of the illusion that is life on Earth. Like you, scientists' interpretations of what they observe in experiments is further limited by their level of awareness of their connection to Consciousness, and many times influenced by their personal beliefs.

Science does not discover anything new, per se. What scientists employ scientific beliefs to discover as new is instead a realization of what already is. Because scientists realize what already is, and their level of awareness of their connection to consciousness limits their understanding of what they discover, they end up with a false sense of knowing. Science does amass and maintain a vast amount of information through its discoveries; however, access to information is not equivalent to knowing what the data is perpetuating.

For instance, there is a plethora of information about how our bodies work, but medical professionals cannot explain or agree on much of it. This disagreement is particularly evident in hospital settings. If you know anyone who works in a hospital in a patient care capacity, you can visit with them to confirm or deny this reality.

What this means is that your most effective method of knowing and understanding anything is by expanding your consciousness on the topic through experience; and even then, there is a chance that your perceptions may limit you. There is nothing wrong with having a false sense of knowing, however, and a quick review of the myriad societal comforts that resulted from scientific studies will prove this. A false sense of knowing is still helping Consciousness expand knowledge of itself. Eventually, scientists correct the false knowing as they expand their consciousness. If you do not believe this to be true, consider that at some point in the past we collectively accepted the Earth as the center of the universe.

Even more important than being aware of the false sense of knowing in science is realizing how the scientists' beliefs and observations affect the outcome of what they study in experiments.

The modifications made to the double slit experiment in quantum physics is an excellent demonstration of this phenomenon. Thomas Young conducted the original double slit experiment in 1801. He published information on the set up of the experiment I am referencing here in 1807. In the experiment, light that passes through two vertical slits creates a wave-like interference pattern on a screen behind the slits. This, in itself, is unusual and unexpected, because you would instead expect two vertical light beams (passing through the vertical slits) to shine on the screen. An even more bizarre outcome of this experiment is that the wave-like interference pattern only occurs if no one or nothing observes the experiment. This is the point I am trying to make regarding how your beliefs affect your earthly experiences. In the double slit experiment, if there is any kind of observation applied to it, the interference pattern disappears, and the light behaves as the observer would expect.

Piggybacking off the knowledge that beliefs and observations affect perceptions of reality, know that scientists in the medical community revere double-blinded, placebo-controlled studies as the gold standard for evaluating the effectiveness of drugs in treating diseases. This is because the study design attempts to shield the results of the study from the observer phenomenon, as well as eliminate any participant, investigator or staff-introduced biases in the treatments being investigated. The double-blinded design seeks to study if the outcome of the experiment resulted from chance or was a result of a specific variable (in this case, the drug being studied).

Amazingly, many double-blinded, placebo-controlled studies demonstrate that, even in the absence of the drug being studied, some patients in the study experience a favorable outcome, just like the patients who received the drug. Not to confuse you further, but there are also some patients who receive the drug and experience an unfavorable outcome. I am not kidding. This means that some patients may be treated with a placebo drug, meaning a drug not containing the active ingredient being studied, and still achieve relief from the illness. Nurses are subject matter experts when it comes to employing the placebo effect to provide relief to patients. They often observe this phenomenon when providing care to patients dealing with pain.

Now, if the drug is not the one providing the relief, what is? Is the phenomenon of chance responsible, or are the patient's beliefs responsible? You will see in Chapter 10 that there is no such thing as chance occurrences, so that leaves beliefs as the guilty culprit. So, yes. I firmly believe your beliefs create your earthly experiences. They can even help you heal your body.

Benefits of Beliefs

So far, I have discussed how your beliefs limit you and prevent you from attaining your desires. I also mentioned how creating and holding onto them is a means to an end for you, as no belief of yours is right or wrong. Instead, they are the catalyst to creating the Earth life show you wish to experience. You can appreciate this universal truth in the example of the patients seeking pain relief and the scientists observing the double slit experiment. In both cases, the patient's and the scientist's beliefs have a direct effect on the outcomes of their experiences.

You can employ this awareness to help you achieve any of your dreams, regardless of what they may be. For instance, if you believe Consciousness has abandoned you and you must protect yourself, then your life will be filled with experiences of fear requiring you to protect yourself. Alternatively, if you continue to believe that you lack the means to meet your ends, you will likely find it difficult to attain any of your goals. Lastly, if you desire to always live in bliss, you can choose to do so by believing that no experience is good or bad and all are a means to an end for you or some other unique expression of Consciousness.

The stronger your desire is to attain a goal, the easier it is to change your beliefs to support you. By the way, just changing your beliefs is far from enough for you to achieve your goals. The new beliefs you create must represent your most authentic, pure, and honest feelings or desires. You cannot lie to yourself that you automatically believe something just for personal gain. You must focus and align your feelings and actions, including your words and mannerisms, in a consistent manner with what you wish to achieve for yourself. This is another universal truth, one commonly referred to as the laws of attraction. Briefly, the laws of attraction perpetuate that if you visualize yourself experiencing an event in fine detail, and then remember and embody the emotional state you achieved by visualizing yourself experiencing the event, you attract the same energetic frequencies in the physical world, which eventually allows you to experience the event (in the physical world). Again, this is a brief explanation of the laws of attraction. However, you may look back at times in your life when you attained what you thought was impossible by ceaselessly obsessing over it to appreciate this phenomenon. In those moments, you were employing aspects of the laws of attraction (either consciously or unconsciously). The laws of attraction are a powerful practice to employ in your daily life, and I invite you to review them to gain a better understanding of how your beliefs shape your world.

An additional beneficial role of your beliefs is to protect you from your fears. Many of the fears you possess result from a trying experience you overcame in the past, and those fears are now protecting you from suffering similarly in the future. Alternatively, you possess the beliefs because some other unique expression of Consciousness developed it after overcoming a trying experience and you are benefiting by simply learning from it (preventing the likelihood of experiencing the same events). Since beliefs keep you safe from your fears, you should be eternally grateful for your ability to create new beliefs at your convenience. This is very powerful knowledge, and I implore you to use it carefully.

Everything you appreciate and accept about you and your life is that way because of your current beliefs. The way the world perceives you is also that way, in no small part because of your beliefs. If you are eternally grateful for the way your parents raised you and you strive to live your life in a manner that would make them proud, you are doing so because you believe their influences were of tremendous benefit to you. If that is the case, know that your parents raised you the way they did because of their fear-based beliefs. I hate to sound like a broken record, but this illustrates how your beliefs are simultaneously protecting and limiting you.

Also, you possess myriad beliefs from this life and previous lifetime incarnations here on Earth, buried deep within your subconscious, that continue to affect everything about your life today. In most cases, you are unaware of their influences.

Deep-rooted Beliefs

You now understand your beliefs are protecting you from fears I have so far explained are illusions. Recall that your fears are your egoic mind's creative constructs brought to life by Satan, and all stem from your continuing to believe that Consciousness abandoned you. Many of these fears and beliefs are lodged deep within your subconscious and continue to influence your Earth life experiences today, without your awareness. These influences manifest as predictable habits you possess that your closest families and friends can use to identify you. In cases where such beliefs are preventing you from achieving your greatest desires or expressing your honest emotions, ask yourself why you continue to hold onto them.

Why do you continue to limit your abilities to be infinitely creative? Truly, if your fears are an illusion, beliefs are no different. They are as much illusions as your fears are, and therefore, are neither real nor permanent. Because Consciousness grants you unconditional love and free will to be anything, any time, know that you can change your beliefs at any moment and not only in certain times. Before you start on a purge journey to replace all your beliefs, however, you must first recognize them and how they are affecting you.

You may recognize them by spending considerable time carefully analyzing your habits. Once you identify a habit that seems odd to you and you are willing to change, question why you possess it. Often, asking five times why you maintain the habit or belief will reveal the subconscious fear or experience you had that caused you to create it. These experiences could originate from your early childhood or a recent, trying event in your life. They could include losing a loved one, going through a breakup, not landing your dream job, or not having enough money to buy what you want. It is important to realize that you are not experiencing any of these events in the present. I mean, today, as you read this book, you are not experiencing many of the subconscious fears that have caused you to be who you currently are (your egoic mind's creation).

Also, I do not mean to downplay who you are today, except to point out that who you currently are is also preventing you from remembering your infinite self. If the deep-rooted fear was going through a breakup with a boyfriend in high school and you are currently married, why are you still protecting yourself from the fear of the breakup?

Imagine how you would react if I showed up to your house to sell you insurance that promises to provide one-hundred percent recovery support if you lost any or all your possessions to a dinosaur attack. That's right. Please imagine if I tried to sell you dinosaur attack insurance. I mean, you are aware of how destructive dinosaurs can be to our current societies. Many shows have depicted the catastrophe dinosaurs would create for humans if we and they were to co-exist in our present societal constructs. You would agree that their enormous size would be of great concern to you and me.

You are additionally aware that dinosaurs no longer exist. They are all extinct. Knowing this, I predict that you would politely decline purchasing my guaranteed best rate offer for dinosaur insurance faster than I can finish pitching the idea to you. Also, you may worry about my sanity or business acumen.

The reason you refuse to buy dinosaur insurance is that the fear of losing your possessions to dinosaurs does not resonate with you. You believe dinosaurs no longer exist and so have no need to buy a solution, in the form of insurance coverage services, to protect you from the fear-based belief that dinosaurs can destroy your possessions. Many of your deep-rooted beliefs lodged in your subconscious are no different from your fears of dinosaurs. What I mean in the previous statement is, you no longer need them.

Why are you still afraid of the dark as an adult? Why do you still think you do not have enough money to do and buy what you want, even though you can buy this book? (Thank you, by the way.) Why do you continue to find it hard to trust people in your life today, even when they have given you no reason not to? Why do you still fear Satan or continue to believe that Consciousness abandoned you?

As you identify your deep-rooted fears and their associated beliefs, place the ones you no longer need in the same bucket you have dinosaur insurance in. As soon as you do this, erase them from your subconscious by returning them to Consciousness, or change them to a belief that will better serve you in your present life. Remember that Consciousness is Energy, and no one can destroy it. Instead, you can only change it from one form to another.

You are hurting no one and nothing by returning your archaic beliefs back whence they came. Instead, as you return them back, you recycle them, and allow another unique expression of Consciousness currently going through the same challenges you faced in the past to access and use to overcome their own trying experiences. This is no different than you donating your notes or textbooks to students currently taking classes that you no longer need to take. If holding onto the notes and books provides you no value, I am sure you would agree that giving them to someone who needs and can benefit from them makes you feel great. I am also sure you would appreciate it if a student ahead of you in school gave you their notes. Alternatively, you could change your beliefs, and by doing so, you are defeating your fears, simultaneously expanding your own consciousness and slowly remembering who and why you truly are. It is a beautiful thing, my friend.

Recap of Your Beliefs are Limiting

Your beliefs are creative opportunities to express who you think you are in the moment. They reflect your current level of awareness of your connection to Consciousness. They help Consciousness expand knowledge of itself.

Your beliefs keep you safe, though they limit the perceptions of your Earth life experiences.

Your beliefs affect and are affected by your duality spectrum, your geographical place of residence, and your experiences. They also give rise to your habits.

Your beliefs are temporary and illusionary, just like your fears. You may change them at any time to support experiencing the Earth life you wish for yourself.

Your beliefs are powerful, and if used correctly, remind you of who you truly are—an infinitely creative being.

Your beliefs are powerful, and, if used correctly, they remind you of why you truly are— to help expand your consciousness, and to support Consciousness' ceaseless desires to create and change.

10

You Are the Actor
and the Director

―――――――――――

"Stop acting so small. You are the universe
in ecstatic motion." —Rumi

I need to applaud you as you continue this journey toward remembering who and why you are. I know you have read a lot of information that must contradict with many of the beliefs you currently hold on this topic. I understand this might confuse your current understandings of who and why you are and want to assure you that this feeling is perfectly normal. In due time, it will all make sense, and my intention for writing this book is to facilitate the process.

You know you are Consciousness, no different from any other thing or any other person that exists except for the frequency of your vibration. You also understand that to experience life on Earth, a choice you bravely and willingly made, you needed to forget who you truly were. The outcome of forgetting this most fundamental aspect of who you are created the illusion of fear that Consciousness abandoned you, further created your ego, and finally, created your duality spectrum. Even as your ego, you understand that you are not an exception to the two rules governing all of life on Earth. Remember, the rules maintain Consciousness in state of balance or homeostasis and bestow unconditional love and free will upon you to do as you please, always.

The quote "with great power comes great responsibility" cannot be more accurate for you now that you understand the responsibility you have to ensure that you experience the type of illusionary life on Earth you wish for yourself. Even more scary is fulfilling your duties knowing that your actions are providing vast troughs of information for Consciousness to expand knowledge of itself. Free will and unconditional love grant you this responsibility.

No one and nothing else will create the type of life you wish to experience for yourself. Only you have the power, at all times, to use your infinitely creative mind to create and experience any sort of Earth life show you can dream of. This is true. The collective experience that represents the current state of affairs of life on Earth is a product of everyone and everything creating or attempting to create the shows they wish to experience for themselves. Regardless of if they are consciously aware of this responsibility or not, everyone, including you, is actively contributing to this reality. Regardless of if you believe it to be true or not, it is what is happening. As co-creator of the universe, you experience the outcome of your wishes and desires, and the actions you engage in to attain them. As both the actor and the director of the Earth life show you perceive, your life situation is entirely your responsibility.

More on the Illusionary Earth Life (Show)

Theatrical shows or movies provide excellent opportunities for you and other unique expressions of Consciousness to experience myriad emotions and expand their understandings of Consciousness. Theatrical shows offer avenues to display the latest, greatest, and most innovative expressions of Consciousness, and to experience inspiration. For example, they showcase futuristic ideations of what's possible through advancements in technology that others can use as inspiration to create in the earthly experiences.

Theatrical shows or movies come in myriad genres, including horror, action, thriller, documentaries, drama, and much more. At different points in your life, you might develop an affinity toward any one of the genres to escape the illusionary reality of your current life situation. You might also gravitate toward any one of them to find inspiration for what your Earth life experience could be. All in all, theatrical shows or movies are great fun, and you and many unique expressions of Consciousness recognize the amount of work it takes to create them.

Creating a show often starts with a thoughtful message or lesson that someone realizes and wants to share with everyone they can reach—often, the more people the better. If the person is not a writer, they collaborate with writers to put together a script, which involves reducing the lessons into writing. The writing is very detailed, providing direction for the actors, the directors, the stage developers, and costume designers on what they must do in order to create the show.

Casting directors review the auditions of many actors willing to portray characters in the show and select those they believe can best bring the characters' roles to life. Many times, the actors undergo additional training on how best to bring the character to life before filming begins. All in all, this and much more must occur before audience members like you and me can see the show.

The director of the show is responsible for coordinating, collaborating, and making the final decisions. It is an enormous amount of responsibility for the director, and I am sure you must be elated that someone was brave enough to take on the duties and responsibilities required to create your favorite theatrical shows or movies.

Interestingly enough, you are well aware that what you see in shows or movies is all make-believe. You know that what you see is not real; what you see is an illusion. The actors bringing characters to life in the shows are not playing themselves. For example, Henry Carville is not really Superman from another planet.

You know how much technology contributes to creating the illusions you watch in the shows and movies. If nothing else, you know that the actors portraying the characters in the shows never truly die like the shows show. If that were the case, you would have entirely different opinions, perspectives, and feelings towards Hollywood.

You know that Hollywood is all make-believe, fake, anything but real, but you are still able to find inspiration and expand your consciousness from watching the myriad shows the industry produces. This is amazing. How beautiful is the knowledge that you can accept that something is entirely fake, and yet rely on it for entertainment, learning, inspiration, and the experience of a wide array of emotions. Is it not magnificent to know that an illusion helps you expand your consciousness? I believe it is.

The point I am reiterating again by bringing this knowledge to your awareness is that life on Earth is not only a dream (as you now know), but it is also no different from the shows or movies you watch. Earth life and all its experiences are entirely an illusionary, fake show. You really could grab yourself a large bowl of popcorn and your favorite soft drink, then sit back and enjoy it as it unfolds.

Just like the movies, the illusionary show that is Earth life also provides you with vast opportunities to teach or learn something, to receive inspiration or experience an emotion, and to enjoy beaucoup entertainment for yourself and all of Consciousness. If Earth life is a show, everyone and everything here must be playing specific roles to keep the show moving on. This is true, and I alluded to this universal truth in Chapter 5.

While playing your role as an actor in the Earth life show, you are concurrently always also playing the role of the director of your show. You are responsible for directing the Earth life show you wish to create for yourself and the role you choose to play in it.

Fulfilling Your Responsibilities

Consciousness prefers that you always fulfil the responsibilities as the actor and the director of your earthly show by expressing your most authentic feelings, emotions, passions, and perceptions. In everything you do, make sure you are primarily honest with yourself as you engage in the actions or behaviors. Even if your purest feeling is based on the illusionary fears you currently believe, continue to always express how you truly and authentically feel. The same holds true for everything that you think and say, and for all the beliefs you create to help keep you safe from your fears. Your truth is all you know, and all you should express, always.

If this is something you only do on occasion, I invite you to begin to do it at all times. You can start practicing by sharing with the entire world how you truly feel about this book when you are finished with it. I mean, you are already an expert on the second rule governing life on Earth, guaranteeing that you can never be wrong. So, there is no need for you to grant your fears authority to stop you from expressing your honest feelings.

As you express your authentic feelings more and more, you will likely experience the illusion of duality in both extremes. This is absolutely fine, and represents an inaccurate understanding of Consciousness maintaining its balance. By the way, as you continue to direct and act in your show, understand that no experience you have, regardless of its outcome, occurs by chance. Chance does not exist, because recall that you and other unique expressions of Consciousness are co-creators of your Earth life experiences and the universes. In the same light, no experience is meaningless. They are always an opportunity to expand your consciousness. Besides, you are also aware that every single experience on Earth is a neutral means to an end for some unique expression of Consciousness. Someone or something wished or thought about it occurring. It might even have been you!

So, keep faith and trust that each experience and outcome is the way it is because it is working to bring you closer to remembering why you are. Consciousness prefers that you always be true to yourself. These are all enormous responsibilities Consciousness bestows upon you, as the actor and the director of your Earth life show. They further demonstrate not only how significant you are, but also how brave of a soul you are to accept them.

Consciousness prefers that you remain honest, and there is a simple reason why.

Consciousness Celebrates Truth/Authenticity

Consider for a minute that Hollywood is a world of its own, and that the Academy of Motion Picture Arts and Sciences is equivalent to the God or Creator of Hollywood. The Academy puts on the Oscars yearly. At the Oscars, the Academy, or the God of Hollywood, celebrates the creativity that the many unique expressions of Hollywood created from the previous year. The unique expressions of Hollywood would include the actors, directors, stage managers, costume designers, and make-up artists, plus many others who all contributed to creating a show.

Before the Oscars event, the Academy reviews all the unique expressions of itself. During the review, the Academy identifies those unique expressions of itself that expressed the most creativity in various categories. For example, the Academy will review and nominate actors who were so creative at portraying their characters that their passion, authenticity, and sincerity were inspiring and almost as real as your perception of your current Earth life experiences. The Academy is seeking those instances of creativity that elicited a myriad of emotional responses from the audience. The portrayals that provided tremendous teaching and learning opportunities for Consciousness. The portrayals that were authentic. Often, the Academy recognizes and nominates five actors for being authentic in their jobs.

Even though only one actor wins the award for being the most authentic at bringing their character's role to life, please recognize how the Academy provides an opportunity to celebrate all other actors, and all the supporting cast and crew who helped the (winning) actor do their job. The actor who wins the prestigious award often dedicates time during their acceptance speech to recognize and celebrate the others. This is because as the actor portrayed their character's role as authentically as they could, they expanded their consciousness and the consciousness of all of Hollywood. This is true.

The actor who wins the award becomes a benchmark for authentic performances that actors portraying characters must meet or exceed for the Academy to celebrate them. This is no different from how Consciousness recognizes actors in the Earth life show.

If your actions and expressions ceaselessly represent your most authentic feelings, you become a benchmark for how all future expressions of Consciousness must strive to act, or surpass, in order to expand Consciousness' knowledge of itself. Do not confuse this information with the thinking that you are less important than some other unique expression of Consciousness. No one unique expression of Consciousness is more important than another. Instead, the information is perpetuating that you focus on always expressing your most authentic emotions and feelings, and to look to others for inspiration. Winning is a natural outcome for when you act in this manner. Truthfully, every unique expression of Consciousness receives this recognition at some point, or at multiple points in their life.

As for the actor the Academy celebrates their authentic portrayal of a character in a movie, notice that the type of character the actor portrayed has absolutely no effect on whether or not the Academy selects them for recognition. The character's role could have either been the protagonist or the antagonist in the show, and it would not matter as long as the actor's portrayal was emotional, authentic, and inspiring. This is true, too!

As you continue to experience life on Earth under the illusion of fear, remember that there is no such thing as good or evil. They are both illusionary constructs of your creative mind. Just like the Academy celebrates authenticity and does not recognize duality, Consciousness also celebrates Earth life authenticity and could care less about your creative constructs of duality. Your ideas and beliefs of a protagonist and an antagonist are as subjective as your ideas and beliefs of a God and a Satan.

Seeking to always be the protagonist in your earthly experiences is great and all, but make sure this goal does not hinder you from expressing your most authentic feelings and emotions. If you continue to seek to always be the protagonist because of a fear-based belief that it is what your creator prescribes, you will ceaselessly experience this same fear in your earthly experiences. Remember, experiencing the same fear is the textbook definition of experiencing Hell on Earth.

On the other hand, always expressing your most authentic and honest emotions and feelings liberates you. It is a guaranteed and practical approach that will undoubtedly help you remember who and why you truly are. Not only that, it will also expand your consciousness, which helps Consciousness expand its own consciousness. Which is precisely why you are.

What-if acting

Even though I stress the importance of always expressing your honest emotions, I understand you may find yourself in situations that require you to pretend, or express made-up feelings and emotions. This is okay when experiencing simulated disasters, or as you train for competition. You should be aware that simulated feelings are also subject to the same two rules and aspects that affect all of Earth life. Simulated feelings do not provide the most effective opportunities to expand Consciousness, but you can appreciate that they are better than nothing. I refer to the act of expressing simulated feelings as what-if acting.

Outside of disaster preparedness or sports training, I truly believe that what-if acting is fear-based, theoretical acting. According to rule number one, this type of acting will elicit an equal and opposite reaction that is also fear-based and theoretical. Sometimes in your Earth life, you may choose to act this way to obtain a response from someone because you wish to test them under the pretense that it will help you overcome your fears. Though fine, this behavior might be detrimental to your personal relationships.

Why? What-if acting fails to provide all the necessary information any unique expression of Consciousness needs to know how they will react. The reaction they express will often not bear any resemblance to their actual reaction. What-if acting is further detrimental because it sets off a series of actions and reactions based on theories. And because you are the infinitely creative actor and director of your show, you are likely to come up with justifications for yourself that convince you the theoretical experiences you discussed with your partner are the actual ones either of you will express and experience. Again, there is nothing wrong with engaging in this sort of behavior, except that you must accept you may not be adequately prepared to experience the action or reaction if the event occurs.

An example of this would be your spouse asking how you would react if you found out they'd cheated on you. *If* signifies the event has not occurred, and because it is a theoretical question, I guarantee your answer would also be theoretical. Many confounding variables are missing from the question, making it impossible to predict what your reaction would be. Because what-if actions and questions are fear-based and designed to tests subjects, this means that as the subject, you are best served by not answering the question. I would implore you to instead focus on identifying the fears evoking this sort of behavior from your spouse and seek to mitigate them.

If your spouse is thinking of cheating on you, there is a reason why. Identifying the reason is more effective than expressing how you would theoretically react if they cheated on you. Fears, presenting as insecurities, are the driving force behind what-if acting.

As the actor and the director of your earthly experience, you overcoming your fears reduces any need for continuing this sort of behavior. It further eliminates the need to continue to deal with the thoughts that evoke them. As an aside, overcoming your fears empowers you to develop and maintain trusting relationships with other unique expressions of Consciousness. This facilitates the provision of fantastic opportunities for Consciousness to expand awareness and knowledge of itself.

Recap of You are The Actor and The Director

You are an illusionary unique expression of Consciousness, meaning you are infinitely creative, you are loved unconditionally, and you have free will to do as you please.

You are solely responsible for the perception of the illusionary Earth life show you create for yourself. This means you are the director and the actor of your show.

You, as the actor and the director of your earthly show, have everything you need to create anything you can imagine, always.

Because of free will, you can choose to change your current Earth life show at any time, into anything you wish. You can cast new friends, family members, and job responsibilities, and you can pick out new props (physical possessions) to work with.

Consciousness prefers that you always fulfill your acting and directing responsibilities authentically, and with your most honest passions and feeling.

Acting and directing are opportunities to create and change, which helps Consciousness expand knowledge of itself. It is also precisely why you are.

Part II-B
Why You Are (After Your Earth Life Experience)

11

Death is Creation & Change — Transformation

"Our death is our wedding with eternity." —Rumi

L et us get right to it. Surely you now understand death, as a fear, is an experience your egoic mind wholeheartedly seeks to avoid. Remember, all the fears and the solutions that your egoic mind creates are to help you survive. They are survival-based fears protecting you from your fear of death. They are protecting you from your fear of not knowing where your soul will end up after your body begins to change. Will you end up in Heaven, enjoying the peace and serenity that your creative mind associates with the place? Or will you suffer the gruesome fate of living in Hell for eternity with Satan?

The above questions are the driving force of your egoic mind's actions, and again, there is absolutely nothing wrong with them—except that your fear of death is no different than your fear of Satan. You fear death because you do not remember the experience, and not because you do not know what it is like to experience it. Death is not the end of your existence as you now believe. Not at all. Death is quite the opposite.

It might be challenging to remember that you have experienced death numerous times throughout your soul's existence. You have likely had many incarnations here on Earth, and the current one is just another of many you are likely to experience after this one. In every one of the incarnations, you experienced death. So, relax, it is not all that foreign to you.

Death is an inevitable part of experiencing Earth life. Nothing is permanent throughout the cosmos, except the permanence of creation and change, or of transformation. Creation and change come in many forms. Death is one of them.

As an aside, you experience a form of death every single night when you go to bed. If this is your first introduction to this knowledge, I am happy to be the one to introduce you to it. You are welcome for helping expand your consciousness. I am also delighted to continue reminding you, you have free will to choose to believe this information or not, and that whatever you choose is all right. You can do no wrong.

There have been many times after waking up in the morning when I cannot remember my night or my dreams. Those deep sleep experiences are a form of death, albeit a less severe one. Sleeping is a form of death because death, which requires the cessation of breathing, also requires that your soul exit your body.

Every night while you slowly drift into deep sleep, your soul exits your body and returns to the spiritual realm. There, it interacts with other beings. As you interact with each other, you sometimes perceive the interactions as basic dreams that you observe passively, lucid dreams in which you are an active participant, or out-of-body experiences where you feel fully present in some other realms. Earlier in this work, I mentioned how nothing happens on Earth by chance. These non-chanced occurrences include the nightly experiences you have, even if you do not remember them. This is another universal truth.

Your nightly experiences are your soul and your spiritual guides providing you metaphoric messages about the fears limiting you from being the most authentic actor and director of your earthly experience. The metaphoric messages also include solutions on how to overcome the fears. Besides that, I am sure you know your nightly experiences also grant you opportunities to experience your most pressing desires.

You know some of your dreams can have a tremendous impact on you, and that some may accurately predict future events. Your dreams contain powerful metaphoric messages, which the messengers prepare and tailor for your sole understanding. Only you can fully appreciate the messages and how to apply them in your Earth life. Interpreting the metaphoric messages requires that you possess a deep awareness of who you are in the moment, including knowing your most pressing desires and fears.

It is not out of the question to enlist wise and advanced souls to help you understand your dreams. The Bible story of Joseph illustrates an example of such a wise soul coming to the aid of Egypt. Appreciate how Joseph's interpretations of Pharaoh's dreams required a deep understanding of Pharaoh's desires and worries. That said, I must caution you to be extra careful when working with a wise soul to assist you in understanding your dreams. I caution you because any interpreter's interpretation of your dream is limited by their level of awareness of their connection to Consciousness, and by their familiarity with who you are in the moment. For instance, in the Bible story discussing Joseph the interpreter, appreciate how Joseph was able to discern the cows represented the perception of time. Some other person may have concluded otherwise. No one can hinder you from seeking assistance to understand your dreams; however, never forgo your own responsibility to understand, accept, and apply the metaphors in your life.

Returning to the experience of death, you know your soul lives forever. It continues to exist even after it exits your body in death. Again, what happens after it exits your body is a notable source of many of your fears because you do not remember. Permit me to remind you.

First, know that death, like birth, never happens by chance. It is always your soul's decision to experience either, and they always happen as they should and when they should. Since you and other unique expressions of Consciousness are co-creators of the universe, there is no such thing as chance. You experience death when your soul decides it needs to change the lessons it chose to learn before incarnating on Earth in its most recent lifetime. You experience death when your soul has learned and taught Consciousness all the lessons it can in its most current lifetime and needs to review its work. You experience death when your soul decides it has had enough of experiencing the illusion of abandonment.

Upon dying, your soul performs a review of your experiences in your most recent earthly incarnation. Your soul performs this review in a place that is void of time, and so you perceive it to occur instantaneously. You learned about the concept of time in Chapter 6, so accepting the idea of reviewing your entire life's experiences in no time should be second nature.

Reviewing Your Recent Earthly Experiences

You currently likely believe that after you die, your God reviews your entire life and judges your actions. You also likely believe your God, based on his judgment of your actions, either condemns you to suffer in Hell or to enjoy peace and harmony in Heaven for eternity. Again, you can do no wrong by believing this; however, I want to assure you it is not what happens. There are numerous reasons why this is inaccurate, and I have touched on many throughout the work.

I can remind you of one by referring you to rule number two that governs life on Earth—unconditional love and free will.

Further, it would be detrimental to Consciousness if unique expressions of itself were not allowed to continue to express their infinite creativity because they were burning in Hell for eternity. Alternatively, burning in Hell for eternity might be another opportunity to expand your consciousness. That said, what I believe happens after you die and your soul exits your body is this: your soul completes a review of its experiences in its most recent incarnation on Earth.

You, as your soul, are the one performing the review and passing judgments. *You* will have your soul guides and other advanced souls assisting you in the process. The guides and advanced souls will only assist, and will do so in a non-judgmental manner. This is a universal truth. *You* are your harshest critic, even in death. As *You* review your most recent experiences on Earth, *You* are evaluating the moments when your acting and directing were authentically reflecting *You*, and when they were not. *You* are evaluating those moments when your acting and directing would have earned you a standing ovation and an Oscar, or not even a nomination. As *You* proceed with your review, *You* take note of the moments when you were either authentic or not. *You* also recognize the moments when you experienced bliss and remembered your eternal connection to Consciousness. *You* evaluate the myriad opportunities you provided that helped expand Consciousness by being true in your acting and directing, When *You* are done with the review, *You* then decide if *You* are satisfied with who you were. *You* decide if *You* are satisfied with the student that you were on schoolroom Earth, and if *You* are satisfied with the actor and the director that you were in the greatest show ever created: life on Earth.

This personal review is another reason why I stress the necessity of always being authentic in expressing your emotions, and of always being true to yourself. Consciousness prefers this; *You* prefer this. If nothing else, always being true in expressing your feelings will come in handy when *You* perform your life review. *You* will feel encouraged, proud, and satisfied with the work that you did.

Your review of your most recent experiences on Earth will also grant you the opportunity to remember who and why you truly are. You will remember when you first experienced the illusion that Consciousness abandoned you. From there, you will become aware of how this illusionary fear caused you to create an ego and was the beginning of all the other fears and solutions that you created and believed would protect you.

You might laugh at the comedy and drama you enjoyed creating for yourself by identifying with duality, especially because you will come to see that everything you did was only a means to an end for yourself. *You* will appreciate the roles that your Satan and your God played for you. *You* will find relief and appreciation as you view the bigger picture of your life – witnessing how every experience, thought you had, word you uttered, and action you partook in was shaping the person your egoic mind created. *You* will relax as you become cognizant of the fact that all you did was contributing to the grand illusionary show that is the Earth life experience. *You* will relax, knowing that it was all a well-designed experience to help Consciousness expand knowledge of itself.

As you continue to review your life, *You* might decide to witness your entire life from immediately after exiting your body back through to the time you spent in your mother's womb. *You* will appreciate how, even in your mother's womb, your experiences were beginning to shape what your perceptions of your Earth life experiences were going to be. *You* will come to understand how your mother's words, actions, thoughts, and surrounding experiences help shape the person your ego thought you were. *You* will finally understand why your perceptions, influenced by how much you were aware of who you truly are, represented what you considered to be your truths. *You* will finally understand and witness that what you believed was what you experienced as the co-creator of the universe.

Another exciting aspect of your life review is *You* will be able to observe it from multiple vantage points. Back to being your true self, Consciousness, *You* will do more than see, touch, taste, smell, or hear the experiences. *You* will become an intimate part of all of them, including becoming part of the other unique expressions of Consciousness who interacted with you. *You* will become aware of their fears and desires and how they also influenced the perceptions of your interactions with each other. *You* will witness how each of your beliefs limited your interactions and led to misunderstandings between you and others. *You* will become aware of moments when your intentions were in sync with others' in your experiences, and how that enabled you to create new beautiful, unique expressions of Consciousness together.

For instance, *You* may recall the feeling of winning a championship or overcoming a challenge with teammates. *You* could also choose to witness moments when your spiritual guides were trying to communicate with you, and how they worked with "Satan" to ceaselessly bring your fears to life. *You* will become aware of the illusion you believed to be Satan and appreciate that the character was always the outcome of your creative imagination. *You* will also become aware of the balance that exists in all experiences on Earth and throughout the entire cosmos. *You* will especially understand how duality affected the perceptions of this balance by creating the illusion that it favored certain unique expressions of Consciousness over others. *You* will reunite with your soul guides and could choose to have them answer any of your burning questions. The fact is, the possibilities of what *You* can do in death are also infinite.

Seriously, death is fascinating! Even more fascinating is the fact that you need not die any time soon to remember the experience. Many souls living on Earth today have gone through the experience partially, and have returned here to Earth to tell us about it. I encourage you to read or watch video interviews of these brave souls discussing their experiences.

Since they died—or better yet, crossed over to the soul realm—and then returned back to Earth, we call the experiences Near-Death Experiences (NDEs). In your spare time, watch or read about NDEs to help yourself remember what the feeling is like. If nothing else, I am confident it will help you become less fearful of death. The less you fear death, the closer you are to remembering your eternal connection to Consciousness and the more authentic you become as the actor and the director of your earthly show. A review of multiple NDEs reveals an underlying message of love and acceptance beyond what words can describe. I believe this love is the unconditional love Consciousness grants all unique expressions of itself, the second rule governing the entire cosmos.

Decision, Decisions, Decisions!

After completing the review and conferring with your guides and other advanced souls, your soul may decide to reincarnate on Earth to play the game all over again. This time, however, your soul may choose to learn different lessons, express different emotions, and create new solutions to overcome newer and increasingly complex fears. Your soul will do all this while simultaneously providing opportunities for Consciousness to expand its consciousness.

The new lessons may be entirely different from the ones your soul learned in its most recent incarnation. For instance, if in its most recent life, your soul was an unfaithful wife, it may now choose to experience life as a husband married to an unfaithful wife. Note that upon reincarnating, your soul will do so with access to all the knowledge Consciousness has gathered since it began to be aware of itself. At any time during its incarnation, you may decide to access the information to support its current endeavors. This is also true for you today.

Alternatively, your soul may decide to incarnate in another realm and experience life as an entirely different being. Think alien races from different parts of the galaxy. If experiencing life in any form does not resonate with you in the moment, you may choose to return to Consciousness. Returning to Consciousness is not the same thing as you might currently believe returning to Heaven is. Remember, the idea you have of Heaven is the epitome of your illusionary construct of peace and harmony. If you continue to believe that Heaven exists, you must also believe that Hell exists (opposite and equal). The truth is, and you should be aware of this already, both live in your mind and are uniquely your own creations.

Again, there is nothing wrong with you continuing to hold onto these beliefs that are the outcome of your illusionary fears; however, returning home to Consciousness is an entirely different experience. Returning home means returning whence you (and everything and everyone) came. Remember, Consciousness is much more than the God you believe in or the Satan you fear. Consciousness is much more than your perceptions of right and wrong or good and evil. Consciousness is much more than your idea of Heaven or Hell. You would be returning to everything and nothing. I have no words to describe what that feels like.

Heaven is Likely Boring

I know, I know. If I struck a nerve with this subheading, you should take the opportunity to authentically express your feelings about it. Consciousness expands most effectively that way, and it supports your ability to act and direct in the Earth life show you envision for yourself. Plus, you should be getting used to this by now. It is not the first shocking heading you have read. I do, however, encourage you to continue reading further to learn why Heaven is likely boring.

Consider how you would feel if your earthly experiences were void of the illusion of fear that Consciousness abandoned you to protect yourself. Mull over what your earthly experiences would feel like if you could, without any challenges, struggles, or opposition, manifest everything your creative mind could imagine. Please do not confuse this with the fact that, while on Earth, you can manifest anything your creative mind can imagine. There is a difference with both. While on Earth, you have everything you could ever need to manifest anything you can imagine. On Earth, unlike in Heaven, there is the illusion of opposition as you manifest your desires. What I am requesting is that you consider the feelings you would experience if you were able to do anything, with anyone, at any time, and as many times as you wished, void of the illusion of fear.

I am confident such earthly experiences will evoke feelings of uneasiness, disenchantment, or even boredom from you. You will most certainly feel like your goals are worthless if you can attain them with ease. As a matter of fact, you may feel hollow and empty on the inside, void of emotion or the ability to celebrate attaining your goals because you would have overcome no challenges in the process. You may even begin to feel as though your life lacks meaning or purpose. You will realize how attaining your goals void of fears provides measly opportunities, if any, to expand your consciousness —to learn.

This feeling is no different from the dread you feel about returning to a job that offers you the same predictable challenges day after day. The dread of dealing with the same challenges you could overcome in your sleep, with meagre effort. In your Earth life experiences, when your job or life situation offers you no challenges to overcome, your infinitely creative mind starts identifying challenges on its own. At your job, you may become annoyed with your coworker's work ethic, mannerisms, or whatever else you can think of. In other words, when you perceive your experiences to be void of challenges or fears, your egoic mind instantly seeks or creates more illusionary challenges or fears to overcome.

To provide additional proof of the universal truth that you are addicted to overcoming challenges—in other words, to creating and changing—I am sure you can relate to the fact that in your current Earth life, you are not comfortable with unwavering support. You struggle to accept unwavering support for your endeavors, even from your closest family and friends, either consciously or unconsciously. When you experience this sort of event, you create challenges for yourself by questioning the support. You may question your friends' and families' motives for being supportive, wondering what they want in return. Same thing happens at your workplace. You already know why this is the case.

Your insatiable desire to continuously seek out and overcome challenges and fears is an essential part of experiencing Earth life. It is an inherent part of being a unique, albeit illusionary expression of Consciousness, which you most certainly are. This seemingly insane behavior is also a firm reminder that Earth life is more about your experiences and the lessons they provide than it is about attaining your ends. If you particularly enjoy solely reaching your ends without challenges, you are currently experiencing life in the wrong place. Your egoic mind might continue to make you believe you dislike challenges, but now you know it is not true. Because you are on Earth during these times, and you came here willingly, accept that you are a brave soul, and that you crave challenges.

Unlike Heaven, Earth offers a plethora of opportunities for you to experience and overcome an infinite array of fears in an infinite array of life situations. Earth offers you the opportunity to attain your goals by overcoming challenges, thereby providing you with a feeling of worth and purpose—even though the feeling is only temporary. The temporary feeling pushes you to ceaselessly attain your heavens as you overcome your hells. This endless cycle is one of the reasons why you chose to come to experience life on Earth. This makes Earth a likely more exciting place to experience life than you probably appreciate, given your current level of awareness of your connection to Consciousness.

You are addicted to challenges, my friend. Heaven offers no fears and no challenges like here on Earth. I mean, there is no Satan in Heaven. When you perceive your Earth life experience to be void of challenges or fears, you are likely to experience a feeling of boredom or lack of excitement or motivation. Life in Heaven is no different than your Earth life when it is void of fears or challenges. And because life in Heaven is void of challenges or fears, Heaven is most likely boring.

Consider this additional explanation for why Earth is likely more exciting than being in Heaven. Consider that you enjoy consuming different forms of media because they allow you to escape to something you perceive to be more exciting than your "real" Earth life, even though you know they are illusions. Media—be it movies, YouTube, Instagram, or Twitter—offers you the opportunity to live vicariously through other unique expressions of Consciousness. Like the illusions that you consume through media, I have explained to you how your Earth life is no different. Your Earth life experience is also an illusion.

So, if the media you consume, an illusion, is more exciting than your "real" Earth life, then, your "real" Earth life, also an illusion, is likely more exciting than what you consider to be realer, Heaven.

This point should further make you appreciate why there is such an allure about coming to Earth. An allure that even you cannot resist. I mean, I am sure if I asked you where you were before you were born on Earth, you would be likely to say, "Heaven." Good.

If you were in Heaven—enjoying your experiences with God and the angels, living void of fear, challenges, sin, your frenemy, Satan, and never needing to worry about dying—why in the world would you accept to leave? Not only that, why would you accept to leave and come to Earth to experience the exact opposite of Heaven? Wait, there is more. Why would you accept to experience the exact opposite of Heaven, knowing that there is even the slightest chance that you might leave Earth and end up in a worse place, Hell, where you will suffer for eternity with Satan?

After considering the above questions, if you continue to stand firm that you made the decision to incarnate on Earth, believing that those were your options, you need to seriously evaluate your ability to make decisions for yourself. The truth is, you came to Earth because it is a simulation, an illusion, and therefore, likely more exciting than Heaven. Also, it provides you the opportunity to play a beautifully designed game, whose outcome is the expansion of Consciousness.

It amazes me that many people who continue to live under the illusion that Consciousness abandoned them spend most of their Earth life wishing to return to Heaven. To be fully transparent, I was one of them, and I understand why it is the case. As students on schoolroom Earth, we are all in different grades. I say that to let you know I appreciate the necessity of the lessons in elementary school, even though I no longer need them. Someone, somewhere, is benefitting from the lessons. Soon enough, they will also move on to grade school, and eventually college. While in college, there will no longer need to return to elementary school.

Today, I understand there is no need to long for Heaven. As I mentioned earlier, you likely believe you recently and willingly just came from there. Know that you are a brave soul and it is not by mistake that you are here on Earth. And as you continue to experience Earth life, it is best for you to be fully immersed in the experience. Your current incarnation is one of many in your soul's lifetime, and I am sure there will be more. You know you cannot deny or downplay the allure of Earth life, just like you cannot deny or downplay how addicting the experience is. If you do not believe me, that is absolutely fine, too. It is inevitable that your next experience of death will remind you of Earth's allure, and of its addicting nature.

Recap of Death

Death is a form of creation and change, two constant activities that happen throughout the cosmos.

Death is not new to you. You have experienced death in the past and do not currently remember it. This is by design.

Death provides you the opportunity to review your most recent incarnation on Earth. From the review, *You* will discern how well you played the game.

Use death as a reminder to always be authentic, so that *You* are proud of your work during the review process.

Do no fear death. It is merely a transition into another form of existence after Earth.

Your ideas and visions of Heaven exists in your mind only.

12

Beyond Earth

"If you do not prepare now for the afterlife,
then when will you do so?" —Al Ghazali

As you continue to experience Earth life, make a conscious effort to reconnect with your soul or remember the eternal connection you have with everything. You will eventually remember, either in death or by using the tools I share in Part 3 of the book. There is no need to worry that you will run out of time. You are an eternal being on your own unique path to remembering. You best assist the process by being authentic in all your earthly experiences. You are aware that Consciousness always rewards authenticity and truth. This is because authenticity and truth provide the most effective opportunities for expanding Consciousness.

As you live your life being authentic and true, you are learning many facets of the infinite intelligence that is Energy, Oneness, Consciousness. You learn how best to work with the Energy in order to manifest your greatest desires and bring to life your wildest creative wishes. The possibilities to work with or change Energy are endless.

The Bible story of Master Jesus illustrates a great example of how any unique expression of Consciousness can become so adept at working with this Energy. The stories provide great inspiration for what is possible. Knowing this, you should be able to appreciate how and why nothing is impossible to create or do. There are infinite ways to do anything, and being creative requires that you leverage your uniqueness to find a path to attaining your means that is true to you. This is precisely why your earthly experiences offer you infinite opportunities to create both fears and solutions ceaselessly. The opportunities are also fabulous for learning and preparing for your work in the afterlife.

If you remember your eternal connection to Consciousness during your earthly incarnation, you may die when you no longer have earthly desires. This is because your ability to experience Earth life from a state of bliss will render overcoming your fears as stressful as a walk on the beach in Costa Rica. After your soul reviews your earthly experiences, you may decide to return with all the knowledge you amassed and play the role of a guide for other souls still on their paths to remembering. Alternatively, you may decide that you no longer need to return to Earth, and instead want to experience Consciousness from an entirely different perspective. Again, the perspectives available to you are infinite. In one case, you could partner with other souls who have attained an awareness and understanding of Consciousness like you, and create an entire world for yourselves to oversee. You could oversee an Earth-like planet amongst the stars in the galaxies. Later in the chapter, you will learn that you already do this on Earth, today, on a smaller scale.

Right now, on Earth, you are a student in school, preparing to graduate. After you graduate, you need to go into the real world, the cosmos, and show Consciousness what you learned. Before we discuss that, I would like to briefly mention the power of your thoughts and their role in such an endeavor.

Do Not Take Your Thoughts Lightly

In Chapter 9, I discussed how your beliefs are simultaneously limiting and keeping you safe as you experience Earth life. The idea that your thoughts are powerful is essentially a reiteration of the information I discussed in that chapter, except a step above your beliefs.

Recall that your beliefs create the world that you perceive. Well, your beliefs are products of the thoughts and experiences that you have. All your Earth life experiences provide you with opportunities to manifest your thoughts in the physical realm. Your entire life situation in its current state is a result of the thoughts you created or identified with.

Earth is one place in the cosmos where you can change the frequency of vibration of Consciousness from thought-form vibrations to physical vibrations. As the actor and the director of your earthly show, you used your thoughts to create the show you are currently experiencing. Everything that you possess, including your fears, beliefs, physical possessions, friends, family, members of your social circle, and your job all originated first from a thought you had. Upon identifying the thought, you latched on to it, believed in it enough, and overcame any fears that might have hindered you from experiencing it as you manifested it in the physical world. Feel free to take a moment and review your current life to realize how it is the outcome of your thoughts.

You are reading this book right now because you thought about doing exactly this at some point in your life. From thought, you were able to manifest it in your Earth life at this moment.

The notion that everything in existence and every experience taking place on Earth originated first from thought further explains why nothing you experience is by chance, and every earthly experience is a means to an end for some unique expression of Consciousness. Somebody or something somewhere thought about experiencing whatever it is you witnessed. Even the reaction to what you witnessed, which is designed to maintain Consciousness in balance, also originates from thought. The current state of the world is as a result of the collective thoughts and desires of Consciousness.

I stress the importance of acknowledging the power of your thoughts because they are preparing you for your afterlife experiences. Thought is one method you will have available to you to manifest your desires in the afterlife. I experienced glimpses of this on the Tuesday morning when I remembered my eternal connection to Consciousness. The entire message I received that morning was in thought form. I heard no spoken words, but instead became aware of the thoughts and remembered that they were always part of my knowing.

Today, you can work with your thoughts to witness their power. For example, through practice, you can become an active participant in your dreams, also known as lucid dreaming. While lucid dreaming you can take control of your dreams and direct yourself to do just about anything you can think of, as long as you are authentic in your desires. These types of dreams are lessons and opportunities to expand your consciousness.

I have had many lucid dream experiences. In one of them, I found myself back in my home country, Cameroon, in a town called Bamenda. I was in the middle of a dirt road in Bamenda, nowhere near any beaches or body of water. After flying around the road for a while, I decided to change the road into a beach, first by filling it with sand. After a few attempts, I succeeded in manifesting part of a beach in my dream. I manifested sand by having it pour out of my right index finger. Even in lucid dreaming, I need to caution that it does take some practice to focus your attention enough to manifest your desires. Authenticity helps. The possibilities of what you can create are endless. Most importantly, they all demonstrate the power of your thought.

You currently use thought to shape the perceptions of your Earth life show and experiences, and it will be no different for your soul after it decides to create its own world, either working solo or in conjunction with other souls in the afterlife.

As Above, So Below

To further help you understand why you will potentially be overseeing your own world in the future and are really the God you believe created you, appreciate that you are creating your own world today on Earth. You and all other unique expressions of Consciousness are all doing the same thing. Even businesses, as unique expressions of Consciousness, are doing the same. You are all playing God. Like the saying goes, "As above, so below." This is true. Your creations differ only in scale, size, and magnitude.

I can illustrate by focusing first on your God's mission, vision, and values. You believe your God has a mission for you while you experience life on Earth. You also believe your God has a vision for what life on Earth should be like for you and all other souls. Lastly, you believe your God has a set of values it expects you and other souls like you to uphold as you work to accomplish its missions and help manifest its vision of life on Earth. You work hard to uphold the values and may sometimes do things that are not aligned with the values. These are examples of when your actions or experiences would fall on the unpleasant side of your duality spectrum. When this occurs, you might believe you need to repent or face consequences for your actions.

Like your God, your favorite business also has a mission, vision and values. Employees of the business uphold the company's values as they work hard to fulfill its missions and help manifest its vision of life on Earth. Appreciate how the company uses its values, or standards of performance, to hold its employees accountable for their actions and behaviors. There are always consequences when an employee's actions are not aligned with the company's values.

Second, I would like to focus on how your God uses unique expressions of itself to make its presence known throughout the world. These unique expressions of itself all play their respective roles as the assist to manifest your God's vision of life on earth. Examples include churches, clergy, the Bible, the Pope, bishops and much more. This is no different from your favorite business that also uses unique expressions of itself to make its presence known throughout the world. These unique expressions include objects and people playing unique roles as they assist in manifesting the business' vision on Earth. Some of the objects or people include company cars, computers, chief executive officer, supervisors, and employees.

Third, I am certain you believe your God will live forever and never perish. You likely believe that someday, the vision your God has for life on Earth will come to be. In the meantime, your God is facing opposition from Satan and other false gods, who are luring many souls away from your God to them. These are souls you likely believe are going to burn in Hell for eternity. Because you are concerned about them, you work extra hard to recruit souls to believe in your God. Again, your favorite business is no different. The business doesn't want to fail. Their leaders also believe they will eventually attain their vision of life on Earth. As your favorite business works to attain this goal, they face competition from competitors who are luring employees and customers away from them.

I hope you now realize that God and Satan are not fighting for your soul like you may have believed. Moreover, I hope you understand that God and Satan are two sides of the same entity. Consider how competing businesses are simultaneously God and Satan, and how this perception is influenced entirely by which business is your favorite. Additionally, appreciate how competition to be the best inspires businesses to be infinitely creative. As they express their infinite creativity, they attract and retain the best employees and customers. Also note how this forces their competition to also elevate their game.

So in effect, everyone benefits. This outcome is no different from what happens on Earth. If you continue to believe God and Satan are fighting for your soul, come to grips with the realization that they are not. Instead, all you and all other unique expressions of Consciousness are doing is helping Consciousness expand knowledge of itself. This is happening throughout the cosmos, no matter how high above or how low below you go.

What Kind of World Would You Create Beyond Earth?

Imagine being responsible for creating and overseeing the operations of an Earth-like planet by your thoughts alone. What would you include as objects on your planet? Would you allow for time to exist there as it does on Earth? What would you permit as behaviors for its inhabitants? Would there be animals and bacteria on your planet? Would there be diseases, famine, or the perception of suffering? What would you provide as a source of energy on your planet? Would your planet have weather? Would your planet allow for souls to inhabit multiple bodies at the same time? Would the inhabitants be able to travel to other planets, or appear and disappear? What would the inhabitants look like, and how would they breathe? What would be their purpose? Would the inhabitants be of multiple sexes like here on Earth? Would men be responsible for birthing children? Would childbirth be pain-free? What languages would the inhabitants speak? As you can see, the questions are endless, and so are the possibilities of what you can create.

Realize how, based on your design, the inhabitants may become aware of themselves and begin to struggle to understand their purpose for existing. I am sure you can appreciate them eventually desiring to know who their creator(s) is or are. I am also sure that, as they struggle to find answers to these questions, you will always be there for them—inundating them with endless love and everlasting comfort to let them know, as unique expressions of you, they are also Consciousness. And as unique expressions of Consciousness, they are always safe and have no need to concern themselves over anything, other than being true to themselves, and in expressing their feelings.

You may also want to remind them that their experiences are providing tremendous opportunities for Consciousness to experience infinite emotions, express endless creativity, and expand knowledge of itself (learn). Dare I say you will be considered a God? Yes and no. No, because the idea of God is limiting. You are Consciousness, just like the inhabitants of your world will be. Yes, only if you continue to believe in your God.

Know that you have always been as magnificent as your God, and it is high time that you remember this information. Life beyond Earth will allow you to continue behaving like the God you currently revere, if you so choose, and understanding this will help you as you journey toward remembering why you are.

Recap of Beyond Earth

You are a student on schoolroom Earth learning who and why you are, and how to work with Energy. In effect, you are preparing for graduation.

Your thoughts are a unique expression of Consciousness, which you should not take for granted. Pay attention to them and use them to help you create the Earth life experience you envision for yourself. This will prepare you for work in the afterlife.

Beyond Earth, you may create and oversee an entire world of your own. You currently do this, albeit to a much smaller scale, on Earth.

13

The Last Chapter

"True freedom is always spiritual. It has something to do
with your innermost being, which cannot be chained,
handcuffed, or put into a jail." —Rajneesh

Take a deep breath and inhale all the prana, chi, or life
force energy you can, then relax as you exhale it all out.
You have made it to the last chapter of Part 2 of the book.
Congratulations, you brave soul. I am sure you have developed a set
of either pleasant or unpleasant feelings from the information you've
just read. This is perfectly normal, and I encourage that you be honest
with yourself about those feelings. Like everything that you experience
or feel, these feelings too shall pass. Recall that nothing is permanent
except creation and change. What you are experiencing as emotions
are providing you vast opportunities to remember who and why you
are, as you journey on your unique path home.

Take advantage of your right to free will and unconditional love to
provide me feedback or reach out for additional discussions on topics

you do not fully understand. I am more than happy to journey with you, as we continue to learn how infinitely amazing we are. Besides, this is precisely why we are here on Earth—to exchange information, which expands Consciousness.

The information I present in this work reflects my current level of awareness of my connection to Consciousness. My understandings and explanations are also limited by my experiences, beliefs, and current fears. Do appreciate that my perceptions are ceaselessly changing as I continue to incorporate being authentic in every aspect of my earthly experiences.

I consider my awakening like graduating with a professional degree from college. Graduating bestows upon you additional responsibilities to go forward in the world and make use of the information you learned. That is why we call graduation, commencement—in other words, the beginning of your work. As you partake in more experiences beyond your graduation, you gain increasing awareness in your field of study. This is no different for me as I continue my meditation practices and continue to assimilate this knowledge in my day-to-day life.

Undoubtedly, I will only improve my understandings of who and why we are, along with my ability to present this information to you. I say this to speak on the power our personal experiences have on shaping our beliefs. To you, reading this information might result in you being aware of more information only. You may still not know or accept these universal truths to be true until you experience or remember the connectedness you share with everything throughout the cosmos. This is perfectly fine, too; it represents your unique path.

Your path is yours and yours only. You are the driver on the road you create as you drive through yet to-be-developed roads. You are co-creator of the universe and can choose to change your path at any time. You did this even before you were born in this current earthly incarnation. This truth explains why nothing happens by chance. Following my remembrance of who and why we are, I now appreciate how all my past experiences were not chanced experiences. They were providing me valuable opportunities to remember. They were also entirely a product of my beliefs, thoughts, words, actions, and fears. I am eternally grateful for all of them occurring exactly like they did. Reviewing them from this new perspective is blissful. My wish is for you to experience the same types of feelings, and soon.

The Nail in the Coffin

A week after my awakening, I was still in a state of both awe and bliss. Heck, I still am in awe today. Not many people get the opportunity to peek behind the stage of this illusionary show we have come to know as life on Earth.

It was early, about 2:00am. I had not slept a full night all week without getting interrupted by one strange phenomenon or another. It could have been a vivid dream, the feeling of some other unique expression of Consciousness in my room, needing to meditate, ringing in my ears, or the return from an out-of-body experience. Waking up consistently at the same hours of the night/early morning, regardless of the time you went to bed, is a common experience amongst individuals going through a spiritual awakening.

Upon waking up on this Tuesday morning, I could hear a distinct ringing in my ears. The ringing continued for another minute or so without changing pitch. I decided to meditate after it dissipated. There were many instances within the last week when my decision to meditate would result in my channeling information directly into writing. Because of this, I made sure to keep a pen and paper next to my bed. At other times, after attaining alternate states of consciousness through meditation, I would access information that I would remember, like I did on the morning I awakened. When I say remember, I mean information I already knew, but had forgotten (by design, of course).

A lot of this information was hardly some new discovery. What I would consider new are the explanations I created to help me present or explain the information in this book.

Anyway, during my meditation that morning, I received information pertaining to the laws of attraction. When I finished, I decided to put it to the test. As the actor and the director in my Earth life show with a new perspective on life, I knew it made absolute sense to finally take conscious control of it. I wrote in my phone exactly what I believed and wished my Earth life show should be, including what role I wanted to play in it. I even included how much Consciousness, playing the role of money, I needed in my show.

After I finished typing it in my phone, I gave it one more pass-through. It was perfect. I loved every bit of what I had written. I then sat up straight in my bed and spoke the words with authentic passion and conviction to the universe. I repeated it three times, for no reason other than that it felt right in the moment. The first two times I spoke the words felt great. Unfortunately, as I spoke the words the third time, I could barely get them out.

A form of fear, guilt, overwhelmed my entire being. I was perplexed that I would develop such feelings in the moment. I mean, why in the world would I be feeling guilty about taking charge of my current Earth life situation and circumstances? As I sat with the feelings a bit longer, I traced the fear to its origin. You'll love this.

Remember I mentioned growing up in the Catholic faith in Cameroon? Remember my teachings of the importance of giving back ten percent of my earnings to the church or to charity to secure a place for me in Heaven? Yes! I kid you not—this was the issue. You must appreciate how twenty-five-plus-years after learning and believing this information, it came to affect me on a Tuesday morning in my bedroom across the Atlantic Ocean. What a deep-rooted-belief! Seriously, I could not make this stuff up even if I tried to. This happens to you also, every single day. Many times, you are not even aware of how beliefs from your past are shaping your current perceptions and behaviors. This is precisely why I believe it is important to analyze your emotional reactions to situations and experiences in your life. This is precisely why I support eliminating your dinosaur insurance-type beliefs.

Anyway, as I became aware of my imminent ban from walking through the pearly gates, I decided to do something about it. Listen, everything happens for a reason, so do not judge my decisions. To ensure I had access to Heaven, I decided I would donate ten percent of my earnings to charity. Like I said, do not judge me for not simply changing the belief. It was my path, and it was perfect, and you will learn why shortly.

So, yes, I decided to donate ten percent of my earnings to charity and proceeded to include this new update in my phone. Just like I did before, I spoke the words describing my new Earth life show with authenticity to the universe three times. And just like before, the first two times went well, and the third time was a dud. I became confused.

In my confusion, my infinitely creative mind figured my decision to donate ten percent to a charity was small. So, I again fixed the problem by deciding to donate not *just* ten percent of my earnings, but *at least* ten percent of my earnings to a charity. I proceeded to express this even newer Earth life show I wished for myself to the universe, but unfortunately, I ended up experiencing Hell again. I went through the exact same experience and ended up feeling like a failure. What a fiasco of a situation!

Before I spoke the words again, I decided I would pick a specific charity or non-profit organization to donate to. Because somehow, I now decided that was what the problem was. My infinitely creative egoic mind decided and believed that not picking a specific charity or non-profit organization was why I could not speak the description of my new Earth life show to the universe three times in a row without feeling guilty.

I struggled to find an organization worthy of my donations, though I did have myriad organizations as options to choose from. I could have chosen to support an organization in Cameroon, any of my alma maters, or the beautiful hospital that employed me at the time. For whatever reason, I found it impossible to decide on any of them. So, instead of choosing one, I thought I would continue expressing my desires to the universe, and the right charity would come to mind as I spoke the words.

As I attempted a fourth time, I could barely finish the first couple of words before I stopped smack dead in my tracks, with my mouth wide open, sitting as still as the stump of a recently cut tree waiting to be rooted. The same knowing and feeling that overcame my entire being a week before came over me again. I can best describe the experience of communicating with this knowing as telepathic communication. No one says any words, and you just know what they want to tell you. It is a one-of-a-kind experience. Oh, I would be remiss if I did not mention how much of a hilarious, sarcastic smart aleck the knowing is. I can only paraphrase what I remembered (received) this time, and here it is.

It began by asking, "Roland, who do you think you are?" It continued, "Who do you really think you are and why are you so quick to forget the lessons and the teachings you remembered (received) a week ago? Do you not understand? Consciousness is everything, and everything that exists is an individual manifestation of this same Consciousness. There is nothing that exists outside of it, and neither you nor anyone else can separate it from itself.

"So, if you decide, as a unique expression of Consciousness, to leverage your rights to unconditional love and free will, and to use your infinitely creative mind to create the Earth life show you wish to experience for yourself, then proceed as you wish. If you wish to experience your Earth life show by receiving abundant Consciousness expressed as money, this, too, is your wish, and it shall come to be. How you choose to spend the money is also entirely an exercise of your free will. And regardless of how you spend it, remember that, to Consciousness, you can never be wrong.

"Understand that if you decide to give all the money to any charity of your choosing, the charity itself is also a unique expression of Consciousness. If you follow this universal truth logically, realize that you would be giving the money back to where it came from—back to Consciousness. Even if you decided to spend the money on a brand-new car, another unique expression of Consciousness, you would still be giving the money back to the same source whence it came. You would additionally be supporting the creativity of other unique expressions of Consciousness who designed, manufactured, and sold the brand-new car to you. You could even put all the money in the bank and never spend it, and you would still be returning it to Consciousness.

"Regardless of how or where you spend the money you earn, under no circumstances will you not be returning it to Consciousness, the source whence the money, you, and everything that *is,* originated. Roland, as everything is a unique expression of itself, it is impossible to spend or share any form of it, outside of itself! Why continue causing yourself stress by trying to find a charitable organization worthy of your contributions? You can do no wrong. Therefore, it matters not where, when, how, or with whom you share Consciousness. Stop thinking you can game the system. You cannot!" And with what felt like a sigh of frustration from having to repeat itself to me two weeks in a row, the knowing left. I remembered again.

The knowing left me in a state of more shock and awe than when it initially began communicating with me. I never thought I would experience the feelings of awe or being in shock to this magnitude in my lifetime. I sat in my bed this time, as still and frozen as a corpse. I had tears running from both my eyes down to each of my cheeks and onto my arms and my palms folded over my laps. This was the second time I'd cried in a week.

After half a minute or so, I began to laugh hysterically. I had not stopped crying, mind you, so you can imagine how ridiculous I looked. This was the second time I'd cried while laughing in a week. There I was, shedding tears and laughing hysterically, because I had gained an entirely new perspective and understanding of the Earth life experience. This spiritual experience was the nail in the coffin for me, putting an end to all the doubts I ever held, or will ever hold, about the magnificent power and meaning of unconditional love and free will, who and why we are, and our roles while experiencing life on Earth. Seriously.

Anyway, because I was laughing and crying at the same time, some of my tears got into my mouth. I could taste the salt in them. I do not remember ever tasting such bliss.

Conclusion

I am honestly proud of you for making it this far. I know I have introduced many concepts and ideas in this book, some of which were new to you, and a lot of which you were already aware. I hope that as you read through, you were able to piece together the information to create a more comprehensive understanding of who and why you are. You must understand that all our perspectives are tunneled and limited views of a larger connected system. Be it religion, science, school subjects or what have you, we all have only limited views of a much larger and connected system.

You and everything that exists, including things you can subject to any of your five senses and your thoughts, are unique expressions of Consciousness. In other words, everything is a unique expression of itself. There is nothing outside of Consciousness, and that is why it is essentially playing or interacting with itself. I mean, why else would Consciousness interact with itself if there was something else to interact with?

Consciousness has and always will be. Consciousness is Energy, which is always vibrating. Its frequency of vibration changes how you perceive it and how it manifests in the physical plane. In its current state, Consciousness is always in balance and perfect.

Consciousness ceaselessly wishes to learn about its infinite self, meaning, it wishes to experience itself as infinite frequencies of vibration. It wants to experience itself as emotions or forms of expressions or manifestations. For this to happen, Consciousness enlists your expertise. Consciousness offers you its unconditional love and grants free will to do as you please. It is the most effective method for Consciousness to fulfill its infinite desires.

My friend, I hope after reading this book, you are now much more familiar with the universal truths that have been around since the beginning of time. I hope you now understand that the universe is ceaselessly presenting you these truths in all your earthly experiences. I hope you can begin to appreciate that you have always known these truths as pieces to a puzzle you have yet to put together. I hope you are now much closer to finishing the puzzle than you have ever been.

My friend, I hope after reading this book you remember, or are closer to remembering, your infinite creativity. I hope you remember that you are a significant piece in a system that is much larger than you can even imagine. I hope you remember that your infinite creativity is a gift that you possess, and that you are free to express it as you wish while you continue to experience life on Earth. Also, I hope you now begin to act authentically in all your earthly experiences.

My friend, I hope you begin to appreciate that all of Earth life is an illusion. There is no reason for it to be something else. If you continue to believe it is more than an illusionary show or school, realize that the belief is merely a reflection of your awareness of your eternal connection to Consciousness. Also, remember that your awareness is neither right nor wrong and only serves to help you create the perception of the Earth life show you experience. I hope you now are aware that all your experiences are as they are to help bring you closer to remembering your true self, and to help expand Consciousness. I hope you now know that it is inevitable you will remember this connection.

My friend, after reading this book, I hope you begin to remember time is no factor to Consciousness. Time not being a factor implies that you might remember who you truly are in either your current earthly incarnation or in one of many earthly incarnations you will experience in the future. Regardless of the earthly incarnation in which you remember this connection, ensure your actions always evoke your honest and purest emotions. I hope you now know that Consciousness rewards authenticity. Also, I hope you understand that the outcomes of such actions are indiscernible, both for you and for Consciousness. I can assure you, you will enjoy your efforts when *You* are reviewing your experiences in death.

Speaking of death, I hope you now are less fearful of the experience of death, my friend. I hope you understand it is an unavoidable form of creation and change, the two constants in the entire universe.

My friend, after reading this book, I hope you understand you may choose not to believe anything you read to be true; however, I hope as you do, you realize how your beliefs, including the ones buried deep within your subconscious, are influencing the perceptions of all your earthly experiences. Know that at any time, you can change your beliefs to support the earthly experiences you wish to have for yourself. Besides understanding your beliefs and their effects on your perceptions, I also hope you now appreciate the effects of duality on your earthly experiences.

My friend, I hope after reading this book, you can now find calmness in your heart and can relax in your skin, fully aware that while on Earth, everything is always perfect in its current state. I hope you never forget that as you are, you are perfect. Your ever-changing life situations and experiences are no different—they are also always perfect in their current state.

My friend, I hope you realize you always have access to everything you will ever need to create anything you can imagine.

I want to sincerely thank you again for reading this book. Remember, you are pure Consciousness. *You* always have been, and *You* always will be. Your earthly experiences are that way primarily because you are a brave soul who chose to experience Consciousness under the illusion that you were separated and left alone to fend for yourself. You are doing this simply to help Consciousness know itself more and more.

If you do not believe this, the most important information I hope you begin to understand is that no one and nothing else is responsible for your perceptions of your earthly experiences. Similarly, no one is responsible for your salvation. All your ideas of Heaven and Hell are in your mind. You need no saving except from your own infinitely creative mind. You are all you need to remember that you are purely Consciousness — to be saved.

I wrote this book hoping it resonates with you and perhaps helps you to adopt a new perspective of your Earth life experiences. I hoped that this new perspective might catapult you further on your path to remembering these universal truths. Everything about you in your current life situation is perfect, and it is that way because you are own your own unique path home.

Thank you for the myriad lessons you provide Consciousness.

Thank you for being a brave soul.

Part III
How to Remember

14

Simple Tools to
Help You On Your Journey

"The one who learns and learns and doesn't practice is like
the one who plows and plows and never plants." —Plato.

All I needed was five minutes in a dark room to begin my journey
toward remembering the universal truths I've shared with
you in this book. Five minutes was all it took for me to begin
to eventually remember who and why I am, and my interconnected
relationship to everything. Surprisingly, I began the journey with
an entirely different intention in mind: I'd hoped to find a coping
mechanism for the stresses I experienced due to my work and school
responsibilities. You can imagine my pleasant surprise when the outcomes
far exceeded my expectations. Picture a kid exploring a safe playground
for the first time. That is what my experiences with meditation were like.

Every day, every session, and every moment I spent meditating was
an adventure that did not cease to amaze me. I still experience the

same feelings of awe and wonderment today. And all it took was five minutes; time I initially believed to have been a waste because it was all I needed to fall asleep from exhaustion after I sat to listen to my body and breath the very first time. Five minutes was all it took to change my life; time you likely perceive as not enough to do anything of value for yourself. Today, as I write this sentence, I am living proof that five minutes is more than enough time for you to begin your personal journey toward remembering this information for yourself.

There is no one right way to remember. Inevitably, you will remember—either while you are alive or after you experience death. Myriad souls throughout humanity's history have employed many tools to help them remember this information. What is certain is that everyone has access to this information, and if you are willing, you will eventually tap into the knowledge and bring it to your conscious awareness. In my experience, three techniques and tools have helped me on my path.

Meditating

There is nothing I love in this world more than meditating. Hold on a second. That sentence is inaccurate, and I apologize for writing it. The following sentence is the more accurate one: besides my wife, there is nothing I love in this world more than meditating. I am who I am today entirely because of my meditating practices. This entire book is as a result of my meditating practices. My constant state of bliss is a result of my meditating practices. My physical being is as it is today, in no small part because of my meditating practices. To name a few benefits meditating has awarded my physical being, I no longer suffer from debilitating dry eyes requiring an endless supply of artificial tears, and my shoulder blades no longer pain me, either. I'll elaborate on the latter benefit.

In the last quarter of 2015, after I graduated from business school, I was still living in the grey world that led me to start meditating. In the three previous years, I'd spent many hours sitting in front of a computer at work, at home, and at school. My posture was far from ideal, and as a result, I developed a sharp pain between my shoulder blades. I was convinced I had a pinched nerve that needed surgical intervention. I remember researching solutions to relieve the pain online. One solution required that I wedge a tennis ball between a wall and the spot on my back that hurt, then slide up and down the wall to massage the spot. I attempted this in vain. I also spent many hours and a lot of money scouring Groupon deals for every type of massage available in the city. That did not work, either. In desperation, I scheduled an appointment with my physician, who then scheduled an MRI for me.

The MRI was scheduled for a Wednesday morning. Wednesday mornings marked the end of my weekly graveyard shifts, the beginning of a week off, and my fighting to recover from a jet-lagged feeling. After a while, I stopped trying to overcome feeling jet-lagged and found it better to sleep through the days and be up all night. Anyway, when I got home from work that Wednesday morning, I took a shower and returned to the clinic for my appointment. I was emotionally, mentally, and physically exhausted.

MRI machines are extremely loud and have very small spaces for the patients to lie in. In the machine, patients must remain still as it (the machine) makes images of their body. To assist, doctors often prescribe the patients sedatives to take before the procedure. In my case, I declined to take any, as I did not think I needed them. I was too exhausted. I remember the imaging technician telling me to do my best to remain motionless throughout the procedure. I acknowledged his instructions, knowing it would not be an issue for me. I promptly fell asleep right when the procedure began. I was so exhausted that the MRI's repeated loud banging noises did not bother me. Besides remembering the technician's instructions to remain motionless, I also remember him waking me up to tell me it was over. Two days later, on Friday morning, I received a call from my doctor telling me my MRI images were normal. I was not surprised by her news. She recommended that I begin physical therapy. I told her I did not need to. She insisted that I begin and went ahead to set it up for me. I never went to a single physical therapy session. By the time I received her phone call on the Friday morning, my back pain was gone.

See, on Thursday morning, I was up around five-thirty. I remained in my bed a while longer and then decided to meditate. I had no desire to meditate for an extended period, but I ended up meditating for three hours straight—from around six to nine that morning. Before this day, my meditative practices had never been longer than thirty minutes. Often, I would fall asleep, or my kriyas, which I discuss below, would scare me into stopping. It was also during this meditating session that I was first exposed to the powerful healing properties of prana, which I also discuss below.

During the three hours, my body performed many series of kriyas, moving all over my bed involuntarily, but in a controlled manner. I got out of my bed on several occasions. While out of my bed, I danced. I used my hands to tap different parts of my body as though I was playing drums. At the same time, I chanted weird, non-comprehensible sounds I had never heard of or uttered before. I sweated heavily throughout the process. My breaths oscillated between fast and slow, and deep and shallow. On several occasions, I returned to my bed, moved around on my sheets, and then got out of my bed and returned to the floor. I stretched different parts of my body, focusing primarily on my back between my shoulder blades. Believe it or not, I also took bathroom breaks.

Right before the three-hour mark, I was back in my bed. This time, I was lying on my stomach and oscillating from side to side on my right and left arms. Suddenly, a powerful urge to move overcame my body. I heard six to seven powerful and deliberate taps on my bed and was thrust into the most intense downward-facing-dog yoga pose I had ever been in. The taps were my hands hitting the bed as they raised me off my stomach and pointed my hips to the ceiling. I tightly flexed the muscles in my arms, my legs, and my hips. It felt as though I was trying to lift a weight with my arms that I was barely strong enough to handle. It also felt as though I was trying to stretch my body so that my butt would touch my ceiling. I held the posture, fully flexed and shivering, for about seven seconds before deciding to stop.

In the moment, I had no idea what had been happening to me over the last three hours. The entire time my body was performing all these movements, you need to understand they were involuntary. I literally only observed as my body thrashed around my room, albeit in a controlled manner. The downward-facing-dog yoga pose was the final straw for me. I was too scared and perplexed to continue.

My breathing was heavy and rapid when I stopped. I turned the light on and sat on my bed. My body and parts of my sheet were wet from my sweat. In my confusion, I was keen to notice the pain between my shoulder blades was gone. I could hardly believe it. I called my mother to tell her, but she did not understand what had happened to me. I called my girlfriend, who was in Germany at the time, but she, too, could barely comprehend the experience I had just had. None of us knew or could explain what had happened. All I knew was, my shoulder blades no longer hurt. That's why the doctor's revelation about not finding anything unusual in my MRI did not surprise me. It is also why I never attended a single physical therapy session. None of this, and so much more, would not have been possible without me meditating.

There is a plethora of information in the spiritual, scientific, and medical communities touting the benefits of meditating. Study after study in the scientific and medical communities concludes that meditating provides tremendous benefits to the practitioner's physical health and wellbeing. Meditating has been shown to provide benefits to blood pressure control, chronic pain management, depression, insomnia, stress reduction, substance abuse, and much more. The practice is very old, dating back more than five thousand years. It is also becoming increasingly prevalent today, as more and more people are employing it to improve myriad aspects of the lives. The Centers for Disease Control and Prevention (CDC) published data stating that between 2012 and 2017, the number of adults who attempted to meditate increased from 4.2% to 12.4%. Meditating is gaining popularity, and I can understand and appreciate why. It provides boundless opportunities for holistic self-care—care for your body, mind, and soul.

So, What Exactly is Meditating?

Most people I talk to picture a practitioner in bliss when I begin to discuss meditating. They envision a practitioner in the lotus positing chanting 'Om'. This is an advanced stage of meditating, and just one type. It is also the outcome of many hours spent doing the practice.

To me, meditating is focusing your mind on one thing or experience for an extended period. The longer you spend focusing on the thing or experience, the more insight, wisdom, and creativity you glean about the experience, which helps you understand who and why you are.

There is no one right way to meditate. You can perform a simple Google search to realize this truth for yourself. There is, however, an effective way for each individual to meditate. In other words, there is an effective way for everyone to begin to understand who and why they are. Since a simple type of meditating practice benefitted me, I will share the type with you next.

How I Recommend You Meditate

To appreciate how I recommend you meditate, you must remember why I began meditating in the first place. I needed to find a way to cope with work and school stress. Before deciding to try meditating, I came to understand that nothing outside my being (body, mind, and soul) helped me attain and sustain the state of being I longed for. Since this was the case, I decided to focus my search away from outside of myself, and instead toward my body, mind, and soul.

Before you begin meditating, you must also perform this elimination exercise. Reflect on what you are looking for and what tools, practices, or activities can help you attain it. If you have attempted to employ many practices, activities, and tools and have not been able to attain your goal, it might be time to try meditating; however, you cannot engage the practice of meditation half-heartedly. It is best that you are fully immersed in the practice; if not, you will fail to reap the full benefits it can provide you. Additionally, you will not attain your goals even while meditating. On my website, www.rolandachenjang.com, you can access a simple tool I created to help you decide if it is time for you to begin to use meditating to help you find what it is you seek. I encourage you to use it. Remember, no tool is any good when not used.

Back to my decision to focus solely on my being: realize that this decision also meant I used no props or additional tools when I began. I did not want to listen to any guided meditations, use any mala beads, chant any mantras, or ascribe to any current traditions or teachings. I personally perceived these established tools or methods as something external of me. I have since come to understand that this was the right decision for me. I recognize that it is a harder meditating practice to master, but it is also the most effective.

First, it teaches you meditating skills that you can use anywhere at any time without needing to pack anything extra. You can practice this form of meditation at home, on a break at school, at work, during a layover at the airport, or while on vacation. There are no limits to where and when you can use it. Second, it helps you understand that you are all you need to remember who and why you are. You need nothing else. Third, beginning with nothing but yourself allots you the flexibility to add any tools in the future. There are also no limits to what you can add to enhance your practice when you are ready to take it to the next level. Fourth, this form of mediation is free. It is not necessary for you to purchase anything to begin the practice.

Below are steps to perform my simple, favorite, most effective, and go-to method of meditating. I do this practice every day.

Step-by-Step Guide for Effective Meditating

Find a quiet place where you can relax sitting upright with your feet flat on the floor and hands resting on your lap. You may choose any other comfortable position. I highly recommend you sit upright, as lying down may cause you to fall asleep. As you advance in your practice, you may begin by standing up. Your kriyas will eventually put you in the position to provide the healing you need most in the moment.

Take a deep breath, in through your nose into your belly. Make sure it is a proper breath. A proper breath moves the air in through your nose and into your stomach. As this happens, your diaphragm contracts. This causes your belly to expand outwards and the air proceeds to fill your lungs. This practice is important, as you will come to see when I discuss breath-work later in this chapter.

Close your eyes. Repeat step 2 above a couple more times until you begin to feel your body relax.

With a relaxed body, let go of actively breathing. Begin observing your breath as your autonomic nervous system takes over. Right now, you take about 24,000 breaths per day, and you barely notice or control any of them. This is the secret to my favorite form of meditating. It requires that you no longer ignore your autonomic nervous system. Instead, it implores you to wholeheartedly pay attention, without interfering, to your autonomic nervous system — specifically, to your breaths. Only observe or notice their creations and changes to their rhythms and sounds. Only observe and notice how they transform your body movements. This simple process of observing yourself represents the beginning steps to finding all the answers to all the questions you will ever ask yourself.

If you struggle to observe your breath, you may choose to observe another component of your autonomic nervous system, your heartbeats. Your heart beats about 120,000 times a day, and you barely notice or control any of them, either. In meditation, I ask that you simply observe your heart beats without interfering.

Keep observing either your breaths or your heartbeats for any length of time you feel appropriate. I highly recommend you continue to steadily increase the amount of time that you spend focusing your mind in this manner. First, it improves your ability to effectively meditate. Second, it allows you to increase the amount of prana, chi, or life force-sustaining energy you expose your body to. The more prana you expose your body to, the more healing occurs. I discuss prana, life sustaining energy, in more detail below. Currently, I spend about two hours a day, on average, meditating. This is a long way from the five minutes I started with.

I also highly recommend that you meditate early in the morning, or during the day. The more alert you are when you meditate, the more beneficial the meditation. If you meditate toward the end of your day, or while you are tired, you are likely to fall asleep. Do not let that discourage you, though. Falling asleep while meditating provides healing benefits to your body.

The above steps describe how I began to meditate. As I spent more time meditating, my experiences puzzled me. They were fascinating and unbelievable. They were literally out-of-this-world. Nothing in my life leading to the beginning of my practice prepared me for the experiences I was having/perceiving. After each out-of-this-world experience, I would perform research on the topic to try to understand it better. I found that the experiences, perceived as physical manifestations, varied just like the number of unique expressions of Consciousness all over the globe. Different schools of thoughts had different names for each of the experiences and physical manifestations. The experiences could also be confused with many illnesses associated with western medicine. The myriad experiences are what I currently understand as kriyas. They often occur as a result of exposing oneself to limitless unadulterated prana, chi, or life force energy.

Kriyas

Meditating allows for the integration of *You* and you. It is also an effective method of returning your body back to a state of homeostasis or bliss. While meditating, you raise your body's frequency of vibration by eliminating your conscious and subconscious fears. As you continually eliminate your fears, you are integrating more with *You*, which raises your body's frequency of vibration. This means you either have to change or eliminate the lower frequencies. The process of changing or eliminating lower frequencies of vibration from your Earthly being (body and mind) manifests as physical symptoms that you perceive and experience. These physical manifestations that you witness or perceive while meditating are types of kriyas.

You are already aware of many of the kriyas I have experienced; however, I want you to know that they are many more types. By meditating, you can experience kriyas as the elimination of gas by belching or farting. Yawning, crying, tearing up, laughing, chanting, speaking in tongues, dancing, moving your body in rhythmic fashions from head to toe, adopting myriad yoga postures, connecting different parts of your bodies, flexing different muscles in your face, stretching different muscles in your body, increased breathing, elevated heart rates, flexing any of your muscles, feeling tingling sensations in your arms, feet and hands, experiencing cold or warm sensations, and even developing rashes are all examples of kriyas. Mudras, or involuntary finger movements, are also examples of kriyas. This list is far from exhaustive.

The most important thing to note about kriyas are this. They are all involuntary body movements. They are also highly controlled, and occur with an intelligence that is both beautiful and serene. At first, they can be distressing and scary. Personally, I thought I was possessed with a demon when I started to experience kriyas. This is because the only reference point I had for similar types of movements was movie clips of exorcisms I had watched. Today, knowing what I know, I can only smile at those thoughts. So should you, especially after reading this book.

Another reason you experience kriyas, besides that they result from integrating more and more of *You* with you, is that, through meditating, you expose yourself to the unlimited supply of pure, unadulterated prana.

Prana

Prana or chi is abundant life force energy. It is the energy that supports and sustains every unique expression of Consciousness. It is the high-frequency vibrational energy and intelligence that helped you become a complex unique expression of Energy from a simple sperm and egg. It is the energy that supports a seed's germination and growth into a large tree, eventually producing its own fruits, leaves, and other seeds. Prana, literally, is life-sustaining energy. All unique expressions of

Consciousness throughout the cosmos are always inundated by prana. All unique expressions of Consciousness also store prana in different forms. Best of all, it is free and abundant. We can never run out of prana. Many eastern cultures refer to it as chi (qi) energy.

To help you better understand what prana is, think of it as the energy you receive after eating a meal. Just like you, the meal you ate needed prana to grow. It would not have been able to grow without the help of prana. Also, just like you, the meal holds prana in a different form. I'll refer to this changed form of prana as adulterated prana. Please understand that my use of the word *adulterated* here does not mean *bad*. It only signifies that is it changed from its purest form, which is abundantly available as it inundates all of Consciousness.

Consider an apple. You derive pranic energy from eating an apple. The energy you derived from the apple is adulterated prana, or apple prana. This prana, though adulterated, is able to help sustain your current state of being. Unlike unadulterated prana, it is limited in how much it can change or heal your being. The more you change any food item from its original source, the more you adulterate the prana you receive from the food. In the same light, if you consume prana that has gone through many "middlemen," the more adulterated it is. This explains the allure of eating organic, raw, uncooked, and non-processed foods to maintain your body in a more pristine state. It also explains, in part, why eating animals isn't necessarily good for you. You receive adulterated prana through the process.

Think of the food chain right down to the original source of edible energy. If you ask yourself what sustains the edible energy, you'll arrive at pure, unadulterated prana. This same pure, unadulterated prana is always available to you. The more you expose your body to this form of prana, the more healing, or creating and changing (transformation), your body experiences. This transformation is what occurs when you attain alternate states of consciousness through meditation.

In deep meditation, your breaths direct prana to flow throughout your body. As it encounters blockages (emotional fears stored as tight muscles or knots in your body), it heals them. The healing releases the low vibrational energy, which in turn causes you to experience kriyas. Sometimes, the kriyas arise as a result of prana flowing to parts of your body that require the most acute attention and healing. In my example earlier, my shoulder blades were an immediate area of concern that received pure pranic energy.

Myriad types of kriyas and exposing your body to abundant unadulterated prana are two overarching experiences you will have when you meditate. How they present themselves and how you perceive them will differ for each person. This is a good time to caution you about maintaining a healthy meditating practice. As you meditate, do not let "experience envy" affect your practice. I firmly believe that no two people will have the exact same experience. So, do not meditate because you are seeking experiences for yourself that some other person had. This is unhealthy behavior, and it will only frustrate you. Meditate with no attachments. Only observe yourself, and I guarantee that your experiences will amaze you. Spending even five minutes meditating regularly will have a tremendous impact on your life as you continue to expose yourself to higher frequencies of vibration. Today, I am proud to say I am addicted to meditation and to exposing my body to excess amounts of pure, unadulterated prana.

I invite and encourage you to visit my YouTube channel, where I share tons of information on meditation. Also, on my website, www.rolandachenjang.com, I have simple tools you can download and use to help you create and maintain a meditating practice that is right for you.

Breath-Work

Besides meditating, I enjoy incorporating breath-work as a powerful and helpful tool as part of my journey. Sometimes while meditating (observing without interfering my breath), my breathing spontaneously changes to mimic breath-work-type breathing. Breath-work breathing is pause-free breathing. It requires no breaks between your inhalations and exhalations. Instead, it requires that you maintain constant air flow between your inhalations and exhalations. The biggest value breath-work provides is maintaining a high amount of prana in your body. From your earlier readings, you are now aware of the benefits of prana as an intelligence that is activating and healing your body from within. The activating and healing are essentially raising your energetic vibration.

As you release low vibrational energy, repressed emotions can come to your conscious awareness. Often, these are traumatic events that you buried deep within your subconscious for good reason. Re-living them can be traumatizing; therefore, it is best to practice breath-work incrementally and for short amounts of time. This gives you a chance to process any emotions that may arise that you are not ready for. I also recommend having someone around you to help you stay calm in case the emotions are too much for you to bear by yourself. You can continue to do this (have someone with you) until you are comfortable dealing with any traumatic experiences that you might remember.

I discuss having someone around *until* you are comfortable with the experience because you eventually *will* become comfortable. You can speed the process by remembering that everything on Earth, including your emotions, are illusions. In order words, the emotions that arise while meditating or performing breath-work are not really happening to *You*, even though you can perceive them as real. Especially if they are past emotions, understand that they are not happening now. If you can learn to observe the emotions that arise and discern the lessons they intended to teach you, you will greatly improve your healing through your breath-work practices. The same is true for your meditating practices.

For more information on everything breath-work related, I invite and encourage you to contact R. Christian Minson. Christian is an international speaker, trainer, and coach, and he is the founder of Breath-flow Wellness, a transformational holistic health business. Christian was a monk for ten years and now spends a great deal of time as the leader of the Breath-Work program at Rythmia Life Advancement Center in Costa Rica. You can also learn more about his work, and breath-work practices by visiting his website, https://www.rchristianminson.com. I have personally worked with Christian and have found his practice to be beneficial.

How to perform breath-work

Find a place where you can lie down with your back raised at about a thirty- to forty-five-degree angle. Keep your head straight above your shoulders and your hands relaxed on your sides. You may use pillows to prop yourself up and help support your back.

You can perform breath-work exercises quietly or incorporate music to your practice to aid you in maintaining the breathing rhythm. You can find free playlists on Spotify, YouTube, or even SoundCloud. Simply search for breath-work holotrophic music.

After getting in a comfortable position, close your eyes and relax your hands on your sides.

Open your mouth widely and relax your throat. Now perform an active proper inhalation that contracts your diaphragm, extends your stomach, and fills your lungs with air. Let your body naturally return to its normal state by passively exhaling the air. At the bottom of the exhale, repeat the proper inhale. Repeat the cycle of active inhalations and passive exhalations without pausing. Try to maintain this flow.

To help you maintain excellent air flow, you may cut a water bottle just below its mouth piece. Insert the mouthpiece into your mouth and create a seal with your lips. Make sure your tongue doesn't cover the opening by relaxing your throat. Perform the active inhalations through the mouthpiece.

Repeat the breath-work exercise for as long as you are comfortable.

One thing I must add here: doing breath-work and meditating practices are always better in groups. If this not feasible for you, it is fine to do them by yourself. More often than not, I have performed these practices by myself and still found them beneficial.

Plant Medicine

The last method or tool I would like to share as an option to help you on your journey towards remembering who and why you are is plant medicine. Plant medicine, often taken as part of a plant medicine ceremony, is becoming increasingly common in the western hemisphere. More and more people are partaking in the ceremonies as they read personal and life-changing experiences that other practitioners share online. It helps that there are more facilities and centers offering opportunities to partake in the ceremonies around the globe, even in the United States. You can perform a simple Google search to read reviews of these centers and ascertain more than enough information to help you decide which might be suitable for you. Often, travel or ceremonial costs are the limiting factors.

How the medicine works is up for debate. There is limited scientific literature on the subject, particularly because one of the plants ingested during the ceremonies contains a compound that is illegal in most western or developed countries. Moreover, plant medicine is more attuned with the ideas of folklore or traditional medicine. Shamans would be the best sources for explaining how the medicine works. Of course, their explanations are limited by their beliefs and fears also. For instance, some practitioners, today, do not allow women on their cycle to partake in the ceremonies they host, while others are fine with it.

In my limited understanding of how the medicine works, I can say it allows you to experience life as the illusion that it truly is. It grants you the opportunity to experience a form of death. It lets you perceive yourself as the illusionary separate being that you are. It shows you how your actions simultaneously affect all of Consciousness. Finally, and please understand this isn't an exhaustive list, it also expands your consciousness so that you are able to perceive other frequencies of vibration not available to you in your regular, more familiar, state of being.

For instance, I was able to observe the stars as living entities (which they are, because everything is alive). I also observed that between the stars are interconnected highways that allowed for the transfer and exchange of information. How the stars shared the information is similar to how we use wifi to connect devices here on Earth. As I watched the stars under the influence of plant medicine, I noticed that each star would send out a signal that looked similar to the wifi signal image we have become accustomed to. It was a beautiful experience, and one of many life-transforming experiences the medicine provided me.

Besides giving me the opportunity to experience different frequencies, plant medicine also validated the information I received on the day I awakened. It confirmed the universal truths I have shared with you through this book.

A stark difference between meditating and plant medicine is the transfer rate of information. Meditating is a like water slowly dripping from a broken faucet. Over time, the water can easily fill the entire sink. This rate of information transfer facilitates your ability to assimilate the information in your everyday life, without losing touch with what you may consider to be real or not — your personal foundation. On the other hand, plant medicine is a like a broken dam. The transfer rate is overwhelming, which may result in information overload. This can pose a significant challenge in your attempts to assimilate back into your "real world" when you return. I truly believe that my consistent meditating practices aided me tremendously in my plant medicine ceremonies. Because of that, I recommend that you develop and maintain a consistent spiritual practice before partaking in plant medicine.

There is one place that offers the opportunity to partake in plant medicine ceremonies that I would recommend for you. When you are ready, I encourage and invite you to book a week at Rythmia Life Advancement Center in Costa Rica. The center is specifically designed to provide you the most loving environment to support you as you journey back towards remembering your most authentic self. As an added bonus, the center is a five-star luxury resort. Seriously, there is no place like it in the world. The staff, the pets, the food, the grounds, and the personalized service are well worth the trip. While there, you can meet R. Christian Minson, who leads the breath-work program at the center. You can also meet the founder of the center, Gerald Powell, whose life was transformed by plant medicine. His personal story of how he ended up overseeing Rythmia is fascinating and filled with tons of inspiration.

As a chronic meditator with a vast amount of spiritual experiences that included healing my back pain, healing my dry eyes, countless out-of-body experiences, astral travel, lucid dreaming experiences, and remembering who and why I am, I had very high expectations for what other lessons I would learn at Rythmia. After a week there, I can sincerely say I was not disappointed. I received more than I expected during my time there. I also connected with lifelong friends on the same journey as me. Since my return, I have spent time encouraging anyone on a spiritual path to make the trip and experience their own personal miracles.

I will reiterate here that I recommend you actually begin a spiritual practice that you can maintain fairly consistently before partaking in any plant medicine ceremonies. You will get the most value out of the experience if you can become comfortable observing your illusionary self (your body) without identifying with its sensations, pains, feelings, or your mind's ceaseless chatter. Still, do not let your current ability to observe yourself discourage you from taking the chance to quickly reconnect with your purest self.

Really, there are infinite methods, tools, and paths you can employ to help you remember that you truest and most authentic self is pure Consciousness. The ones I share with you are my go-to, preferred, and proven methods. I love that they are simple, effective, and, for the most part, free. You seriously have everything you need to begin the journey. The only thing stopping you is you.

The End

I am eternally grateful that you purchased and read this book. I want you to know that I am available as a resource, partner, and facilitator to journey with you back home to Consciousness. Together, there is no telling how much we can help Consciousness expand its knowledge of itself.

Here is a thought—why don't you expand your consciousness at this time? What do you think about taking the Connection to Consciousness Assessment again? It would be interesting to find out if your responses have changed, and how much.

My friend, I have always enjoyed discussing and learning about who and why we are. I have no intention of stopping. I would love to hear your experiences and anything you feel comfortable sharing. Expect that you will be hearing more from me again soon. I am as eager as a recent graduate to share with the world what I am learning through my meditating practices and through my assimilating of the information in my earthly life. I can describe the process as more than exciting. It is more than magnificent. It is more than blissful.

Thank you much for your bravery and open-mindedness. Never forget who and why you truly are. You are pure Consciousness. *You* always have been, and *You* always will be. Never forget that your earthly experience is a temporary illusion designed to continue to expand Consciousness' awareness and knowledge of itself. Never forget how valuable you are in fulfilling this eternal desire of Consciousness. Never forget who and why you truly are.

I hope you read this book with joy and in joy.

Thank you and take care.

CPSIA information can be obtained
at www.ICGtesting.com
Printed in the USA
FFHW020656290719
53883144-59635FF